The Divorce Handbook

The Divorce Handbook

Your Basic Guide to Divorce

REVISED EDITION

James T. Friedman

Random House • New York

Random House and colophon are registered trademarks of Random House, Inc.

Library of Congress Cataloging-in-Publication Data
Friedman, James T.
The divorce handbook: your basic guide to divorce/James T. Friedman.—Rev. ed.
p.   cm.
Includes bibliographical references (p.).
ISBN 0-679-77130-1
1. Divorce—United States—Handbooks, manuals, etc.   2. Divorce—Law and legislation—United States—Handbooks, manuals, etc.
I. Title.
HQ834.F74   1997
346.7301'66—dc21   97-19973

Random House website address: www.atrandom.com

Printed in the United States of America
24689753

Revised Edition

To Sol R. Friedman,
divorce lawyer

ACKNOWLEDGMENTS

The author gratefully acknowledges the assistance of his secretary, Pamela Hewitt; his paralegal, Marnie Schloss; his associates, Joshua T. Friedman and Jeffrey I. Garfinkel; his partners, Errol Zavett and Muller Davis; the marital therapists Alan M. Jaffe, Psy.D., and Honey Rosenfeld, LCSW; and the credit expert Bruce Passen in the preparation of this revision and update of *The Divorce Handbook*.

CONTENTS

VIII. FINANCIAL HIDE-AND-SEEK WITH YOUR SPOUSE   56

XII. THINKING SETTLEMENT: NEGOTIATION STRATEGIES AND TECHNIQUES   102

XIV. PREPARING FOR TRIAL   124

LIST OF CHECKLISTS, GUIDES, SAMPLE SCHEDULES, COURT DOCUMENTS, AND WORKSHEETS

The Divorce Handbook

CHAPTER I

Who Needs This Handbook?
How to Use It

1. Who needs this handbook?

Every person who is thinking about a divorce or is in the process of getting one needs this handbook.

The book is designed as a practical guide to take you chronologically through the various stages from the first time the subject crosses your mind to the final decree and closing your file. No one person experiences *all* the steps included in this book, because every divorce differs in the areas of disagreement and extent to which certain issues may be contested in court. The question-answer format allows you to read only what concerns you at the moment. Reading from cover to cover will give you a perspective on the entire divorcing process.

2. Why do I need this handbook?

A major part of the emotional stress of divorce is being involved in something you don't understand. Divorce unleashes fears of material loss as well as feelings of abandonment and guilt, thus clouding your ability to think clearly about financial settlements, personal needs, and the needs of your children.

Divorce places you at the mercy of a system that has its own language and procedures and seems to move people about like pawns from one courtroom to the next.

For example, if you have experienced any of the following predicaments, you need this workbook.

• One day you want a divorce and the next day you want a marriage counselor.

• You don't want a divorce but your spouse just filed for one—or has mentioned the possibility.

• You have just come from your first appointment with a lawyer and he used a number of words you didn't understand but didn't ask him to explain.

• Your spouse is jeopardizing your job with phone calls to your employer and/or lies to your friends and co-workers.

• Your spouse has missed his temporary support payment for the tenth time.

• Every time you call your lawyer you forget two points of the five that you wanted to cover—because she sounds hurried.

• Your divorce seems to be standing still—and you're standing in quicksand.

• With inflation you're bleeding from support payments. Can they be modified?

• Court continuances are ruining your schedule. Doesn't anybody else work?

• Your lawyer is in court or in conference every time you call.

• You never know when you'll see your children. They seem brainwashed against you.

• The silver and the piano are missing.

• You have agreed to too large a support payment and can't manage financially.

• You feel helpless and your life seems out of control.

3. How can a lawyer use this handbook?

By using it with you as a guide at various stages of your case. If, for example, he suggests you review the Hidden Asset Checklist on page 67, you may help uncover assets that never would have been discovered otherwise. Application of your factual situation to the sample trial outlines will enable you and your lawyer to save hours in trial preparation, and you'll both be thinking on the same wavelength. A secretary or paralegal can also use the outlines and checklists to assist you in the preparation of your case at less expense. Lack of communication is the single greatest problem between busy divorce lawyers and emotional clients. This handbook provides you with a common source of communication and should be the basis for your organization and preparation at every stage of negotiation or litigation. Lawyers, give a copy to your clients and ask them to refer to it before asking you questions. They will still have questions, but they will be more focused.

4. How can this handbook help me?

It guides you through the divorcing process step by step and provides perspective—an overview of where you are now and should expect to be later. This handbook puts you in charge of your life at this difficult time.

- It identifies important information relevant to your case.
- It also tells you where, when, and how to find that information.
- It organizes and stores the information in one readily available place.
- It reduces your insecurity and frustration by involving you in the process and showing that you are not alone.
- It helps you select a lawyer and deal with him or her effectively.
- It enables the lawyer to give better answers because you will ask better questions.
- It provides resource information for particular problems through an extensive bibliography.
- It includes a glossary of legal terms common to divorce.
- It's your security blanket—and it covers everything you'll need to know about the divorcing process.
- It puts you in the habit of asking questions. Even if you think you know the answer, ask!

5. Why can't I let my lawyer do it all?

Because he probably won't. And can't.

For one thing, he is too busy to answer every question at length, and for another, you probably won't know the right ones to ask. Your frustration will grow in direct proportion to the court orders, continuances, judgments, and situations you do not understand or know how to handle.

Furthermore, your lawyer should not do it all. It is your responsibility to find and organize the necessary records and documents. Few people—or lawyers—can afford to pay an accountant or other professional just to gather information and put it in usable form for the case.

You should not be a passive participant in your own divorce. You, the client, have a vital role to play in the divorcing process.

6. Why can't my recently divorced friends advise me?

Every divorce case and set of circumstances are different. Your friend may have four more children than you do, or none. She may have a trust fund or he may like the vegetarian life. They may have living parents with a guesthouse, a supermarket in the family, or a brother-in-law who is a plumber. Remember, each divorce is unique—like the marriage that preceded it.

However, you can learn from your friends' mistakes. Do get practical information regarding their settlement agreements—copies of the actual agreements if possible. Ask them: What would you do differently? Would you use the same lawyer?

CAUTION: Remember, friends' priorities are not necessarily the same as yours. They may also have conflicting loyalties to you and your spouse.

7. What does this handbook include?

Basic information on divorce in a question-and-answer format
Practical suggestions and guides
Worksheets and outlines to prepare your case
Checklists
Glossary—so you understand the language
Bibliography for publications that can help you
Sample agreements, court orders, and pleadings
Questions you need to ask yourself and your lawyer
Answers you have to have

8. What does this handbook leave out?

Detailed tables presenting the laws of each state on grounds, property, alimony, and maintenance, child support and child custody, residency requirements, etc. These laws change regularly and require legal interpretation to be fully understood. An experienced local lawyer is the best source for this information.

9. How do I use this handbook?

You can read from cover to cover to get a detailed overview of a contested divorce from beginning to end.

You can look over the Contents when you have a particular problem. Just read the answers or use the checklists, guides, and schedules, listed on page xxi, that concern you at the moment. Determine what information and documents you need. File documents you already have in an envelope. Cross them off the checklist and begin searching for missing documents or other information important to your case. Contact the people who can give you the information or documents you still need. The Internal Revenue Service, your bank, your broker (stock, real estate, and insurance), or your doctor may provide valuable information. Former neighbors or friends might make good witnesses if a trial becomes necessary. Find their present addresses and phone numbers. Mark them down on your Witness List.

In any event, take this book to an early appointment with your lawyer to discuss what may be relevant to your case. Have her review checklists with you and get specific directions as to what she will need and when.

CAUTION: If your case is contested, keep your records where your spouse won't find them. If no safe place is available in your home, keep them with a trusted friend. There is no point in letting the other side know your strategy or how much information you have gathered or lack. Also, it may be a good idea to photocopy and replace documents when you don't need the originals. If your spouse alters or "misplaces" the documents later on, you will have a valuable record and a possible basis for discrediting him or her, which the court calls impeachment.

CHAPTER II

Divorce at Your Doorstep

10. When does the divorce begin?

The divorce begins when you or your spouse first seriously think about ending the marriage. Every married person thinks about divorce or separation from time to time. When these thoughts linger *after* the anger or frustration has passed, they are a signal to *do something* because your marriage is breaking down. When the "I want out" thoughts dominate the desire to work things out and you start considering the practical aspects of separation or divorce (change of residence, living expenses, effect on the children)—the divorcing process has begun.

Once begun, the process does not have to end in a divorce. It is the willingness to do something positive as soon as you recognize the process beginning that gives you the best chance of reconciliation.

11. Should I stay married for the sake of the children?

Probably not, if they are the *only thing* keeping you together. The coldness or hostility displayed by you and your spouse is bad for the children and may even interfere later with their own marriages. In reality, though, people rarely remain together just for the sake of the children. Most of the time there are other factors at play, sometimes unconscious ones.

In fact, other gratifications from a relationship can keep an estranged couple together even though their marriage is dead. Arrangements sometimes develop in which married couples share the household only because it is economically or socially convenient. They create their own separate lives within the home, without interfering with or substantially annoying each other. Parties living in a state of truce for many years will often divorce after the youngest child is independent.

If no such gratifications exist for you, then deal with your marital problem realistically. Don't just ignore the deterioration of your marriage or mope around about it—solve it, adjust to it, or separate. Too much self-sacrifice can be intolerable to your children as well as your spouse.

12. I don't want a divorce. Should I fight it?

Yes, at least to the point where you are sure the marriage cannot be saved. At that point your resistance should be geared only to what's necessary to obtain a fair settlement. Not wanting the divorce is usually a key leverage factor because the party anxious for the divorce will usually *buy* his or her way out—offer inducements to change your mind. Let your spouse induce.

On the other hand, if you overplay your leverage with unreasonable demands or fight the divorce out of vindictiveness or self-righteousness, the result is likely to be economic and emotional devastation for your entire family. Fight only where there's a positive result to be achieved.

13. What can I do to encourage my spouse to reconcile?

The decision to divorce is a way of dealing with one of life's most stressful situations. The decision is usually very slow in coming and has turned into a firm commitment by the time you find out about it. A spouse convinced that divorce is the only way will not be turned around by any magic formula or therapeutic quick fix. Reconciliation is a long process requiring *mutual* motivation to understand what is wrong with the relationship and to do something constructive about it. Because the word "reconciliation" itself is threatening to a person committed to divorce, you might have better luck talking to your spouse in terms of "constructive resolution" of your marital problems. Constructive resolutions can relate to many issues in addition to reconciliation and may not trigger the stonewalling that unwanted focus on reconciliation usually does. Some specific suggestions that may lead to con-

structive resolutions for you and your spouse are found in the Reconciliation Guide on page 165.

14. I want a divorce. Can't I just leave?

Yes, you can, but talk to a lawyer *before* you make this crucial decision.
In a potentially litigated divorce a number of strategic considerations
argue against a spouse's leaving the marital home. For example, if a
wife or a husband seeking custody of the children leaves home without
the children, he or she may be at a substantial disadvantage when the
actual custody proceedings begin.

A physical separation may also have a lot to do with the timing of the
divorce. If, for example, your spouse wants you out of the house but is
reluctant to agree to a divorce, it may be a strategic error to move. Once
you're gone, your spouse's desire to separate has been satisfied and
there is no need to speed along the divorce proceedings. Your spouse
can then obtain repeated continuances of court proceedings or make
arbitrary settlement demands in order to delay resolution of your case.
The more this delay frustrates you, the more of a leverage factor it becomes. You will ultimately pay more or receive less in order to settle
the case. *Refusing* to leave the house when your spouse wants you out
reverses the leverage. The greater the "want," the greater the leverage
that can be employed to achieve concessions in other areas of negotiation.

If you believe there is a genuine physical danger to you or your children, you should either get out of the house or consult an attorney for
a domestic violence Order of Protection. Dealing with domestic violence is discussed on page 13.

CAUTION: In some states leaving the marital home can be construed
as desertion if the statutory period of separation is met. Only when the
departing spouse can prove good cause for leaving can the separation
be construed as "constructive" desertion and provide grounds for divorce for the departing spouse.

15. Can a separation save the marriage?

Sometimes, yes. Physical proximity can be a great source of antagonism for couples considering divorce. A change in the status quo is

often the first step to saving the marriage. The new perspective gained by separation may help you discover the cause of your dissatisfaction. The actual experience of separation provides a testing period that can alter perceptions of divorce as a solution. The party who is pushing for a divorce in the mistaken belief that physical separation will resolve his or her unhappiness often finds that the contrary is true. Separation then may provide new insight into the cause of unhappiness or the advisability of resuming the marital relationship.

16. If I leave the house voluntarily, can I get back in?

The longer you are gone, the more difficult reentry is likely to be if your spouse opposes it. Even if you have a written agreement that says your leaving will not prejudice your right to return, courts are sometimes reluctant to enforce such an agreement if the separation has been long. Very often a spouse who is sincerely interested in saving the marriage will agree to leave in order to give the other spouse an opportunity to reconsider. However, by making such an arrangement, the departing spouse takes a very real chance that no reentry will be possible.

CAUTION: See a lawyer before leaving.

17. How do I get or give financial support during a separation if no court action is pending?

Support is obtained by agreement with the other spouse or by taking possession of marital assets and using them to satisfy your support needs. A joint bank account, for example, is the most liquid asset for satisfying immediate needs, unless you have cash in a cookie jar or safe-deposit box. A charge card is also a handy way to obtain cash or pay for necessaries in an emergency, but an interest charge that can be as high as 18 percent will accrue until the balance is paid. If liquid assets aren't available, some women out of desperation have sold their jewelry or household furniture to put food on the table. In most cases, unless income is clearly inadequate, relief can be obtained from the court before it's necessary to sell personal property. If your spouse can contribute to support but won't, get into court as soon as possible to avoid dissipation of family assets. A nonsupporter will most likely be hiding assets as well.

18. Do voluntary payments set a precedent?

Yes, very often they do in terms of amount. If a supporting spouse has voluntarily been paying $200 a week for an extended period, it may be difficult to convince the court at a later time of an inability to pay that amount, unless there is proof of a substantial change in financial circumstances.

CAUTION: If the supporting spouse is eager to bring the divorce to a conclusion, he or she may inadvertently delay final settlement by meeting *all* the financial needs of the other spouse, who is content to remain in a separated and supported condition. A delicate balance must be maintained in arriving at a support figure before formal divorce proceedings. If this figure is unreasonably low, it provokes the animosity of the other spouse and escalates the contested aspect of the proceedings. If it is too high, it sets a precedent, which raises the level of expectation of the recipient spouse, who will settle for nothing less. A temporary support figure that is too high or too low becomes a leverage factor that will speed up settlement of the case only if the spouse who pays less or receives more than he or she should is also the one who is anxious to settle. That spouse can voluntarily modify the support as an inducement to a permanent settlement.

19. Can I date during the separation?

Casual dating will not legally affect the granting of the divorce, the award of custody and support, or the division of property. However, if your dating involves considerable time spent away from the children or staying out overnight, it may take on the aspect of moral misconduct and can affect some of the issues in your case.

The attitude of your spouse is also important. If dating makes your spouse jealous, the vindictive reaction will certainly slow down resolution of your case. If frequent dating of the same person indicates an intention of early remarriage, you are providing your spouse with a useful leverage factor to reduce your share of the settlement. It is best to consult your attorney before you get involved in any regular or serious dating.

CAUTION: Your spouse may encourage you to date in order to point an accusing finger at you during divorce proceedings. Be careful and discreet.

20. What about sexual relations with my spouse once a divorce is likely?

There is no definitive answer to this question. In states that recognize condonation as a defense to divorce, you may lose your grounds by continued marital relations. You may also delude yourself or your spouse into a false hope of reconciliation through continued sexual relations. Your good sense and your attorney's advice will be required to make this important decision.

21. How do I deal with physical violence?

Call the police or sheriff's office in your community. Although police are reluctant to involve themselves in domestic disputes, they necessarily do so on a regular basis. Criminal charges for assault and battery or child abuse should be brought where appropriate. Your spouse has no more right to physically abuse you or your child than a stranger would have.

Every state has now enacted domestic violence laws that supplement peace bonds and civil restraining orders, which were often ineffective in preventing or punishing spousal abuse. The new remedy is called an Order of Protection, and it can be entered either by the civil court that hears divorces or by the judge hearing criminal or juvenile cases. A divorce case does not have to be pending to apply for an Order of Protection, and persons protected include spouses, children, and any household members. The federal government also prosecutes interstate domestic violence through the Violence to Women Act of 1994.

22. It looks like divorce. How do I protect myself?

See a lawyer as soon as possible. You don't have to hire one, but you must learn what your rights and obligations are in regard to your spouse and your family. There are many books and pamphlets on divorce and separation that discuss property rights, support rights, and custody rights. (Some are listed in the Bibliography at the end of this book.) But *no* book or pamphlet or person untrained in the law *as it applies in your community* can advise you adequately. The written law of your state (statutes) interpreted by your appellate courts, as well as the application of those laws in your local courts, will determine your rights and responsibilities.

CAUTION: This book does not list or discuss particular state divorce laws because no two states are the same, and those laws change every day. A local lawyer can best advise on your local law and appropriate strategy. We emphasize procedures and techniques in the divorcing process that will enable you to ask your attorney better questions and understand the answers better too.

23. How should I deal with my spouse during the divorce?

Divorce tends to bring out the worst in people. Self-interest apparently justifies deceptions and outright lies that would be intolerable to nice people in ordinary times. Self-protection requires a new set of guidelines for dealing with your legal adversary:

1. If love is gone, substitute politeness.
2. Be skeptical. Half of what is said is meant to deceive you. The other half is self-deception.
3. Breast your cards. Don't let your spouse know how much you know.
4. Walk away from arguments or conflict.
5. Expect your spouse to resent your lawyer and to attempt to undermine his influence.
6. Don't enter into private negotiations without your lawyer's knowledge and advice.
7. Don't make agreements or sign anything without talking to your lawyer first.
8. When in doubt, believe your lawyer, not your spouse.
9. Use the lawyers as hired insulators. Learn to say: "Talk to your lawyer and have her talk to mine."
10. Don't rub in your legal victories. Losers try to even up.

24. What are current trends in divorce law?

Divorce law is a pendulum that swings back and forth with the changing trends in society and the traditional family.

1. *Custody for Fathers.* As more mothers enter the workforce and

pursue careers, more fathers are being awarded child custody and child support.

2. *Shared Custody.* There is continued reliance on shared child custody as the favored mediated result.

3. *Custody Caution.* Courts have second thoughts about shared custody awards that are used as an excuse to reduce child support or undermine parental authority. Shared custody is not favored for parents who can't communicate or won't cooperate.

4. *Long-Term Alimony.* The decrease in alimony awards that paralleled the growth of feminism beginning in the late 1960s has been slowed by economic reality. Women in their thirties and forties simply do not have great career opportunities if they have been out of the workforce to raise a family. As a result, short-term rehabilitative alimony is giving way to longer-term awards that bridge the gap in income potential.

5. *Alimony as Compensation.* Alimony is being used to compensate wives who boosted their husband's incomes by putting them through professional school.

6. *Alimony as a Dividend.* Some courts are allowing wives to share in the increased income their husbands enjoy after the divorce as a result of career development during long marriages.

7. *Child Support Collection.* There has been a federally mandated increase in state agencies involved in the collection of child support at no cost to the client. State and municipal laws have been passed denying licensing privileges to deadbeat dads, and income tax refunds are now applied to support arrearages. Ironically, by being denied licenses and public contracts, nonsupporters are losing the ability to pay support.

8. *Support Abuse.* Now that all states have statutorily mandated percentage guidelines for minimum child support, legislatures and appellate courts are concerned about the injustice of arbitrary guideline applications.

9. *Growing Federalism.* Divorce and family law, once the strict province of state courts, is now the subject of federal legislation. For example, Congress has already passed laws concerning child support collection, interstate and international child abductions, postdivorce health insurance coverage for spouses and children, transferability of retirement benefits upon divorce, protection from spousal abuse and domestic violence, bankruptcy protection for support awards, income

tax deductions for spousal support, and nonrecognition of same sex marriages.

10. *Fault Grounds.* Some states are considering the reintroduction of fault grounds as a precondition to marriage dissolution.

11. *Punish Misconduct.* Some states have reintroduced fault to compensate spouses for flagrant marital misconduct.

12. *Interspousal Torts.* Many states have modified their immunity laws to allow spouses to sue each other for physical and emotional injuries.

13. *Professional Civility.* There is increasing pressure from judges and attorneys for greater civility among attorneys acting overzealously on behalf of their clients. Attorneys who don't investigate their clients' false pleadings risk court sanction.

14. *Discovery Abuse.* Divorce court calendars have gotten clogged with onerous and expensive document demands and expert evaluations. The courts are trying to cut through this endless paper chase with tighter time limitations, narrower search parameters, and sanctions for litigants and attorneys who abuse the rules.

15. *Complex Litigation.* New property laws have increased the length and the cost of divorce trials that regularly involve complex tracing and valuation issues. Discovery abuse comes from the degree of preparation required for these cases.

16. *Alternative Dispute Resolution.* Mediation and arbitration are growing in popularity as alternative dispute resolution systems to supplant slow and costly court procedures. Success requires a strong mutual commitment to settlement rather than trial.

17. *Domestic Violence.* Growing public exposure of domestic violence and child abuse has resulted in tougher laws to identify and punish the abusers.

18. *Remarry, Redivorce.* As the American population grows older, second and third marriages are more common and tend to end in divorce more quickly. Elder law is now a viable subspecialty among divorce lawyers because older folks have special kinds of problems.

CHAPTER III

Choosing a Lawyer

25. Can I get a divorce without a lawyer?

In most states, yes. If there are no complications involved and you and your spouse can agree on *every* issue, you can file the necessary papers and enter the final judgment dissolving the marriage.

CAUTION: If you have property to divide, children to provide for, or alimony to pay, you should seek the advice of a lawyer about rights and responsibilities in those areas.

26. Must the lawyer be a matrimonial specialist?

Not necessarily, but he or she must be familiar with the matrimonial practice as it is conducted in the *court where your case will be heard*. If your case has no complex issues or great controversy and no substantial property involved, obviously you have less need for a superspecialist than if your case is potentially complex or contested. A primary function of your lawyer is to give you perspective on the potential results in your case. She must be familiar with the support ranges and property divisions customarily granted in your court at the time. Changing laws and changing judges result in changing applications of the law. Your choice is similar to that offered in the medical profession—if you have a difficult medical problem, you will be more likely to go to a specialist than a general practitioner.

If you suspect that your spouse has hired, or will hire, a lawyer with considerable experience who carries a great deal of weight in the court where your case will be heard, you need a lawyer with equal influence. The consideration your case and your lawyer will receive is very often related to the respect your lawyer can command from the court and the opposing lawyer.

CAUTION: A knowledge of tax law is a *must* where property transfers and support payments are involved. You need a divorce lawyer who can foresee potential problems and make their resolution part of the settlement. Outside tax expertise can be called upon to assist in the resolution if necessary.

27. How do I find a lawyer?

There are a number of ways. First, ask for a recommendation from a lawyer you have used—and liked—in the past. If that lawyer does not handle divorce matters, he or she can refer you to someone who does.

A second source is friends and relatives who have dealt with divorce lawyers. Since no one ever feels like a winner in a matrimonial case, they will frequently refer you to their spouses' lawyers. ("But don't tell him I sent you.") In any event, they can tell you about their own experience with their lawyers and give you some advice on what to look for and what to avoid.

A third source of information is the referral services of your state and local bar associations, which are listed in the telephone yellow pages. Tell them it is a matrimonial case and ask for the names of a couple of people experienced in that area of practice.

Since the United States Supreme Court has approved advertising by lawyers, you can now look to your local newspaper or yellow pages to find a lawyer who specializes or concentrates in matrimonial law. Unfortunately, most states do not certify specialists, and there is no way to verify the truth of any particular advertisement without checking out that lawyer's reputation through the bar association or by asking other lawyers or friends. *A lawyer's reputation among other lawyers is probably the most valid indication of his or her capabilities.*

28. What if my spouse suggests a lawyer?

Be careful. It is not likely your spouse wants you to have the best divorce lawyer in town—or even the fifteenth best! On the other hand, if you have checked out a particular lawyer who seems right for you, don't eliminate him just because of your spouse's recommendation. That could have been the reason for the recommendation in the first place.

29. Can one lawyer represent both of us?

One lawyer can never really represent both parties in a matrimonial action if there are any disputed issues, but it is not always necessary to have two lawyers. If the matter is simple and there are no contested issues, one of the parties can appear "pro se," that is, represent her- or himself. One lawyer draws all the necessary documents and proceeds with the dissolution without the necessity of a second lawyer. You can then share the cost of that lawyer's services.

CAUTION: If regular support payments, questions over custody or visitation of children, or division of property is involved, you should at least have a second lawyer look over the agreement before you sign it. A small change in the weekly support rate can mean thousands of dollars over an extended period. A misunderstanding about your interest in marital property could result in an unforeseen tax obligation, and so on. In only the simplest cases—and perhaps not even then—should you take the chance of going it alone.

30. Should I shop for a lawyer?

Yes, unless you have a referral source in whom you are totally confident. For example, if you have a great deal of trust in your business lawyer, and she makes a very strong recommendation, follow it unless the other indicators are negative. Otherwise, interview at least two lawyers and compare them in terms of competence, personality, and price. The personality factor is important because you will have to deal closely with this individual on potentially volatile problems. While you needn't be totally enchanted, a clash of personalities may make this relationship uncomfortable or even contentious. If your case is a simple one, you may wish to avoid the lawyer who appears unnecessarily contentious. The key test in judging your lawyer's personality is simply compatibility with your own—or at least an absence of *incompatibility*.

31. What about law clinics or publicly supported legal services?

Law clinics are a comparatively new development. The quality of any particular clinic in the matrimonial area will depend on the lawyers and supportive personnel. At such a clinic, your price criterion will probably be met, but you still must consider the lawyer's competence and personality. After your initial interview, if you are satisfied on those points, there is no reason not to hire the lawyer. However, ask whether that lawyer will be the person representing you, or whether it will be an associate or other office personnel. If your case requires personal attention, then you want to know who will be giving you that attention.

The fact that a clinic may advertise divorce for $250 does not mean it won't be entitled to a larger fee if a great deal of personal contact and litigation time are involved in your case. These matters should be clarified at the outset of your relationship with the law clinic or with any other law office. The difference between law clinics and private offices is that lawyers in clinics attempt to minimize *their* hours spent with clients. They maximize the use of forms and the assistance of secretaries and paralegals, who charge at a lesser rate because they do not have law degrees. This approach is satisfactory if the case is simple and does not involve a lot of contact between lawyer and client.

Ask about the hourly charge for the *lawyer* at the clinic. Compare that rate with what is commonly charged in your community and determine whether the clinic is a bargain for *you*.

32. What do I need to know for my initial interview with the lawyer?

Ideally, you should be prepared to describe the extent and value of your property, your monthly living expenses, and the amount of your available income. (See Information Frequently Requested at Your Initial Interview on page 168.)

If this information is not immediately accessible to you, it can be furnished later, and the interview need not be delayed in the meantime.

CAUTION: The lawyer can only advise and predict on the information *you* furnish at this stage of the case. The more incomplete the information, the more vague the advice.

33. Is my interview confidential?

Yes, even if you do not hire that lawyer. Laws and rules of ethics recognize a lawyer-client privilege that prohibits the lawyer from divulging information learned when acting as a lawyer, unlike what is heard in a casual conversation at a cocktail party. Because of that privilege and the confidential nature of your interview, this lawyer will be disqualified from representing your spouse if you do not hire him. Some people have been known to interview the top matrimonial lawyers in their area simply in order to disqualify them as potential representatives of their spouses in later matrimonial litigation.

CAUTION: If your attorney discusses other cases with you in intimate detail or identifies litigants in discussions at cocktail parties or other social events, and if confidentiality is important to you, she is probably not for you. Competent matrimonial lawyers are not gossips.

34. What should I expect of my lawyer in handling my divorce case?

Your lawyer should help you maintain perspective as to what is a fair settlement. She should assist you in discovering all the assets and income information necessary to arrive at such a settlement. She should be prepared to litigate issues that cannot be resolved by agreement, because of either the arbitrary position of the other side or the inability to agree on certain factual questions. You should also expect the lawyer to at least partially *control* the case. She should control you in order to avoid willful violations of court orders or agreements. She should control the opposition by frustrating attempts to take advantage of you by willful or arbitrary conduct. By controlling you and the litigation, the lawyer ultimately presents you with certain settlement options. You have been well represented if you have options to choose from rather than results forced upon you.

Few matrimonial cases are definitive victories or losses. Grays predominate over blacks and whites, and your lawyer prepares you to accept the grays. (And perhaps saves you money in the process.)

Don't expect a miracle or even a stunning victory. The competent lawyer looks for a fair settlement rather than a punitive one. Beware of the lawyer who encourages your desire to get revenge upon your spouse by financial or other means. Also beware of the lawyer who promises you everything. In the emotional context of a marital dispute, you are at the lowest ebb in your ability to make reasonable judgments. If the lawyer gets caught up in your emotionalism, her judgment will be no better than your own. One clear head is better than none.

QUESTIONS TO ASK YOUR LAWYER
AT THE INITIAL INTERVIEW

1. What percentage of the lawyer's practice involves matrimonial cases?
2. Does the lawyer have trial experience in matrimonial cases?
3. Is the lawyer willing to go to court to litigate the case if it cannot be settled?
4. Will the lawyer handle the case personally, or will an associate in his office handle it? (If another person in the office is to be involved, you may wish to have an interview with that associate before retaining the lawyer.)
5. What is the lawyer's procedure for being telephoned at home?
6. How long will it take to resolve your suit *after* an agreement is reached? How long will it take if any matter is severely contested? (In most cases, the lawyer will be able to give you only a general estimate because she cannot control court calendars or the other side's determination either to cooperate or to stall the resolution of the case.)
7. What will the lawyer expect from you in terms of assistance in the discovery process and availability for court hearings, conferences, or depositions?
8. On what basis does the lawyer charge for his services in matrimonial matters? If he uses an hourly rate, what is that rate for office time and for court time?
9. Does the lawyer consider her fees to be average in your community, or above or below average?
10. What does the lawyer estimate the court costs will be?
11. Which spouse will be liable for the fees and court costs? How will that liability be determined?
12. Does the lawyer charge a retainer fee? How much will it be, and is it refundable in full or in part under any circumstances?
13. Can the lawyer give a ballpark estimate on the total fee?
14. Will there be monthly billings or will the fee be due at some particular time?
15. Will there be charges for outside services by accountants or investigators? Does the lawyer charge *extra* for work by his paralegals or secretaries?
16. Present company excepted, whom does the lawyer consider to be the best qualified matrimonial lawyers in your area? (Only ask this question if you are shopping. It is useful if you find that the same name or names come up repeatedly.)

17. Based on the information you have given her, ask the lawyer what results she would anticipate on any particular contested issue in your case either by court decision or by negotiation. (Since predictions are risky and the information you have provided is probably incomplete, you should expect a guarded answer with no absolute assurances of a particular result.)
18. If you are satisfied with the answers to the previous questions, then ask the following: How do local laws affect any issues that may be contested in your case relating to child custody, support, alimony, or property division?
19. Ask any personal questions you have regarding your rights and responsibilities in connection with your spouse, e.g., whether you must prepare meals, pay your spouse's charge accounts, file joint tax returns, etc.

The Bounds of Advocacy, published by the American Academy of Matrimonial Lawyers, provides a comprehensive guide to what constitutes fair play by lawyers and clients in matrimonial cases. A copy can be obtained by telephoning the academy at (312) 263-6477.

35. What if I don't feel comfortable with the lawyer after the initial interview?

That lawyer is not for you and should not be hired. Your time will not have been wasted, because you will have a clearer idea of what you are looking for when you interview the next lawyer. Remember, the initial interview is a two-way street. The lawyer is also deciding whether or not he wants your case. You have every right to be as selective. If you are not comfortable with a particular lawyer, or if you question his competence, you will never fully trust him, and his ability to represent you effectively will be undermined.

36. What criteria do I use to choose a lawyer to represent me?

The lawyer's answers to the Questions to Ask Your Lawyer at the Initial Interview above will aid you in judging her suitability based on knowledge and experience. Your reaction to the lawyer as a person is equally important, because you will ultimately have to trust her judgment. It is hard to trust someone if you have a negative reaction to her personality.

37. At what point is the lawyer retained?

When you ask the lawyer to represent you and he accepts. If the acceptance of that responsibility is conditioned upon your payment of a retainer fee, then his responsibility does not begin until that fee is paid.

CHAPTER IV

Lawyers' Fees
and Court Costs

38. How important is cost in choosing a lawyer?

Lawyers have only so many hours a day to devote to their law practice, so the lawyers who are in greater demand generally charge more for their time. Price is not always a measure of competence, however. In every community there are lawyers whose achievements in public relations exceed their legal skills, who charge more than they are worth. You must first learn the ballpark figure for your type of divorce. (The case where both parties agree is the cheapest, and the contested-through-trial case the most expensive.) Friends who have recently been through a divorce, or else the local bar association, can tell you what the going rate is. If a lawyer you are considering charges substantially above *or* below the average figure in your community, you should explore that lawyer's credentials further before hiring him or her. Although some of the most competent lawyers may charge in the average fee range, few undercharge. A lawyer charging substantially below the norm may lack experience in the matrimonial field.

To put it another way, some of the best fee bargains in the matrimonial field come from young lawyers who make up in dedication what they lack in experience. However, if your case is likely to involve lengthy negotiations and a complicated settlement, or may go to trial, you should not take a chance on inexperience. In the long run, if you can afford the more expensive lawyer who has a good reputation in the matrimonial field, you are probably wise to spend the money. Your lawyer's stature in your local legal community may have a significant effect on the outcome of your case.

39. How do lawyers charge in matrimonial cases?

Most lawyers charge a retainer fee (see Question 44) for taking a case and charge additional fees as the case proceeds or at its conclusion. The retainer can run from a few hundred to several thousand dollars, depending on the lawyer's reputation in your community and the anticipated difficulty of your case. Most lawyers keep track of the hours they spend on a case and bill accordingly. Before retaining a lawyer, you should determine the amount of his retainer fee and the hourly rate that he charges if you are to be billed on a time basis as well. When a lawyer represents a woman whose husband is the breadwinner, he may require her to pay only the retainer fee, with the understanding that the balance of fees will come from the husband or from the wife's share of the financial settlement. In states with community or equitable property division systems, it is common to have each party's attorneys' fees and litigation costs charged against their share of the divided marital estate. If you fire your attorney before the case is completed, only the unused portion of the retainer fee will be refunded, and additional fees will be required if the time already spent on the case justifies it. Hourly rates for matrimonial lawyers will vary substantially, but fees from $100 to $300 an hour are not at all uncommon, and recognized specialists may charge more. In New York City, for example, the fee might go as high as $500 an hour.

40. Who pays the attorneys' fees and court costs?

Many women mistakenly believe that their husbands will pay for the divorce. In fact, whoever hires the attorney is responsible for the attorneys' fees and costs. If your spouse is the breadwinner and more financially able to pay attorneys' fees, the court may require a contribution in the form of temporary or final fees and costs. If your fees or your spouse's are paid from marital assets, they will be part of your division of the marital estate. In effect, both parties contribute to each other's fees by reducing the size of the marital estate to be divided. If fees are paid from your nonmarital assets, the marital estate is not affected.

41. May I ask about the lawyer's fee on the telephone when I make my initial appointment?

Yes, but don't be surprised if she refuses to quote a fee until she has more information about your case. Some lawyers or the secretary with whom you make the initial appointment do quote minimum fees and hourly rates, and you should not hesitate to ask. However, the fact that information is not given over the telephone should not keep you from making an appointment. If you are looking for the cheapest possible divorce, the best lawyers will probably not be interested in your case anyway.

42. Do I have to pay for the initial interview with the lawyer?

Because this varies, you should ask when setting your appointment. Many competent and highly regarded lawyers do not charge for initial interviews. If it is clear, however, at your initial interview that you are *not* looking for a lawyer to *hire* but are seeking legal *information*, the lawyer probably will charge for his time and you should be willing to pay for it.

43. Do I discuss fees at the initial interview?

Definitely. If the lawyer doesn't say, you should ask what the retainer fee will be, whether or not it is refundable, and whether you will be charged at an hourly rate or on some other basis. Bar associations no longer have minimum-fee schedules, but all lawyers have their own criteria, which generally include a minimum fee and an hourly rate.

COMMENT: Many good lawyers are more uncomfortable discussing fees than their clients. The fact that *you* have to bring up the subject does not necessarily mean your lawyer intends to charge a fortune.

44. What is a retainer fee?

This is the fee a lawyer initially charges for taking your case. It is generally not the entire fee. Hours spent on your case may be credited against the retainer fee. If the cost of the divorce goes beyond the initial retainer amount (as it usually does), the succeeding hours are added on to be paid in the manner previously agreed upon.

The retainer is normally not refundable if your lawyer completes your case without using the entire balance. If the attorney's services are terminated before the case is completed, any portion of the retainer fee not used for fees or costs is normally refunded to the client.

45. What are court costs?

In a strict sense, court costs are only those charges made by the court in connection with the filing of the case or subsequent pleadings, and for transcribing the record of court proceedings. In a more general sense, court costs include any costs incurred in your suit other than compensation for the lawyer. This would include investigative fees, expert and appraiser fees, court reporter charges for depositions, subpoena fees, photocopy costs, postage, telephone, and the like. Most lawyers keep track of the costs separately from their fees and present them to you in an itemized bill. When the attorney quotes you a fee, she does not normally include these costs.

46. Should I have a written contract with the lawyer?

If there is a fixed overall fee arrangement or a strict hourly rate charge, a contract indicating the amount of the fees or hourly rates as well as the *specific* services to be performed is desirable. Even a letter or memorandum from the lawyer setting forth the services he intends to perform, and whatever fee information he can provide, is a good idea if no formal contract is drawn. This protects the lawyer as well as the client because the emotional turmoil of matrimonial litigation often undermines the relationship between lawyer and client. The lawyer may want to remove himself from the case later on or the client may want to discharge the lawyer, and it is helpful to have some memorandum that will eliminate any question about the initial fee arrangement. Lawyers frequently insist on such a memorandum if the case appears potentially troublesome at the outset. You should not hesitate to have another attorney review your written fee agreement or memorandum before you sign it. Doing so takes only a few minutes, and the cost, if any, will be negligible.

CHAPTER V

Child Custody

47. When do we tell the children about the divorce?

As soon as you feel that it is inevitable. Don't be surprised if they already know. In the case of a separation, the children should be told at or about the time it occurs. The key word is honesty. Don't hold out false hopes that the marital relationship will continue if it is obvious that it will not. Don't blame your spouse for everything, but also make it clear that the separation is in no way the children's fault. Children frequently blame themselves for their parents' marital problems.

Consult sources in the Bibliography that refer to children and divorce. If you feel unequal to the task, don't hesitate to seek advice from a therapist. Take advantage of the guidance available for you and your children during a period when you both may need it most.

48. How do we tell the children?

Keep it simple and straightforward.
Both of you should tell your children at the same time if your relationship allows that kind of cooperation.
Don't dramatize or become sentimental.
Avoid an air of remorse or devastation.
If you and your spouse have been fighting openly for some time, the

kids may even be relieved that the truth is out—and that the arguments and tension will stop.

Reassure them that you both love them.

Let them have their say—tears, anger, hurt, pleadings.

Let them know with whom and where they will live if that is agreed. If
it isn't, both of you should try to encourage them to express what
they want, while making it clear that they will not have the burden
of choosing or rejecting a parent.

Do not make promises or hold out false hopes of reconciliation.

If there is likely to be a contest over custody or grounds, assure the children they will not have to be involved in the court proceedings—if
that is the case. All children tend to be apprehensive on this point.

Do *not* in any way encourage them to take sides. Eventually, you will
have an ex-wife or ex-husband, but your children will not have an
ex-mother or ex-father.

Assure the children that you both will always be there when you are
needed—if that is the truth.

Read some helpful books on the subject. (See the Bibliography.) Get
professional help for any child who appears unable to cope with the
stress.

49. Do mothers always get custody of children?

No. Although traditionally it was presumed that young children were
better off living with their mothers, most states have rejected this as a fast
rule and many more fathers now seek custody. A mother now must prove
that she is in fact the principal nurturing parent or that, for some other
reason, the children would best be served by being placed in her custody.

A father seeking custody has the same burden of proof. With the
change in traditional male and female roles over the years and the increase in career opportunities for women, it is no longer unusual for
the father to be the principal nurturing parent, both psychologically
and physically. In the great majority of custody cases, it is the past history of caring for the children rather than any sudden rush to become
a superparent during the divorce proceedings that the court will consider in making its custodial determination. A parent who has been indifferent or neglectful isn't going to convince the court by suddenly
becoming attentive and loving.

Today, more fathers are being awarded custody by the courts, sometimes with the mothers' agreement, sometimes against their wishes. If a mother, for example, leaves the state or lives with someone to whom she is not married, or if she is giving her career priority over care of the children, she may lose custody if her husband appears able and willing to act as the principal caretaker.

50. How do I know whether there will be a custody fight?

One of you probably was principally responsible for the day-to-day care of the children. This person, in most cases, would be expected to be the custodian. On the other hand, the question of custody is often used as a smoke screen behind which other issues are negotiated. Awful court battles can result. The children may be used as leverage to achieve an advantage in some other area of dispute such as alimony or property division.

An even worse battle results when a parent contests custody to gain revenge upon the spouse for an unwanted marital breakup. This is striking where it hurts the most without regard to the effect on the children. Greed can at least be bought off with settlement concessions. Self-righteousness almost always leads to an expensive trial whose results may be harsher than either party anticipated.

51. Can the children be used as witnesses?

Yes. If they are mature enough to give reliable testimony, the children are considered legally competent to testify on both grounds and custodial issues. Whether or not they *should* be used as witnesses is another question. The parent who wants a child to testify, or threatens to use the child as a witness, is not giving first priority to the welfare of the child. Testimony in open court or even in the judge's chambers, where it is most often heard, is traumatic to any child, at almost any age. The mere suggestion that the child might have to testify against a parent creates a state of apprehension that may not end until long after the divorce is over. The parent may not be aware of that apprehension, because it is often unspoken. Every effort should be made to complete litigation without using the children as witnesses. They should be assured on this point from the outset to avoid unnecessary fears.

52. What is joint custody?

Joint custody is an award of the child's legal custody to *both* parents, with specific provision made for his or her principal place of residence. Legal custody is the right to make vital decisions regarding a child's education, religious training, health care, and the like. While joint custody was only occasionally used in the past, 41 states have now enacted legislation allowing some form of joint parenting on the dissolution of a marriage. In some states, joint custody is an option available only by agreement. In others, it is the presumed or preferred arrangement.

Many child psychologists and domestic relations specialists discourage joint custody because it can result in a conflict of parental authority, with parents and children in a continuous battle for affection or control. Joint custody can work if *both* parents are more interested in the *children's* best interests than in their own rights. Most divorced people cannot sustain a sufficient degree of cooperation to keep personal antagonism out of this less structured custodial arrangement. Joint custody is definitely not advisable if the parents cannot communicate with each other. Notwithstanding the potential problems, there is a definite trend toward joint custody, and bills have been introduced in every state legislature calling for some form of joint parenting.

53. What is split custody?

Split custody is an arrangement whereby the children live each (or some) with a different parent, or all together with each parent for a portion of the year.

The split-year arrangement is most common when the parents live so far apart that frequent contact for short periods is impractical. The disadvantage is the difficulty the children may experience in adjusting to a new school and social environment every few months.

Splitting the children is usually done only when they clearly prefer it. The mutually supportive relationship of siblings can provide continuity and stability when parents have separated. Those benefits should not be sacrificed as a negotiation compromise or to suit parental convenience. See page 178 for a sample Joint Parenting Agreement.

54. Can the children choose with whom they want to live?

Before any formal court hearing, the parents should give serious consideration to the children's preference. Most parents are not inclined to *force* a child to live with them. On the other hand, if a child's prefer-ence is expressed in court, it will be weighed in light of the child's ma-turity and the reasons for the preference. There is no set age at which a child's preference will *control* the court's determination. It is only one of many factors to be taken into consideration in determining *the best interests of the child*, the universal standard for custodial awards.

55. Should we ask the children with whom they prefer to live?

If they have not voluntarily expressed a preference, the children are probably telling you that they do not want to make the decision. In that case, it is better not to ask directly. However, there are many indirect ways to explore a child's preference. For example, if separation and di-vorce are inevitable, the father may discuss his own future living arrangements with the children. To observe their reactions, he might talk about rooms that could be set aside for them. Unless children are severely repressed, they will generally say how they see themselves in the separated arrangement.

Don't try to manipulate the children's opinion by seducing them with promises of an unreal environment of fun and games. Don't cre-ate a dependency relationship or try to make the children feel sorry for you. The mother who says, "Who will take care of me if you don't live with me?" or the father who says, "I guess you will never see me again after the divorce," is in effect trying to manipulate the children into ex-pressing a custodial preference out of pity. If children choose to live with the pitiful parent, they often play the part of parent and assume many burdens that are inappropriate to their age or stage of develop-ment. Parents who give the children's welfare first priority will not place any of these false expectations or burdens on their children in an effort to influence the choice of custodian.

Bear in mind that, even at its most amiable, divorce is hard on chil-dren. They may not *know* whom they want to live with, they may not want to be asked, they may change their minds, they may continue to hope their parents will get together again.

56. How do courts rule on temporary custody?

The child's best interest is the test for temporary custody, the same as in a final hearing. Generally the temporary motion judge does not have time to grant a full hearing, and the tendency is to leave the child where he or she is until a final and complete hearing. If both of the parents are in the home, the child remains with both. If one of the parents has moved out, the child generally remains with the parent who is in the home. Normally a child has strong ties to school, friends, and activities in that neighborhood, and removal would cause a serious disruption. On the other hand, if there is evidence of potential harm to the child if left with a particular parent, courts will usually grant a hearing on that issue and order temporary custody accordingly.

57. May I leave the state with the children?

Yes, if there is no custody action pending or decree entered. Otherwise, it will be necessary for you to obtain court permission or the approval of your spouse before removing the children from the jurisdiction. That approval should be in writing because the spouse who says yes today may deny it after you have left, and you will incur substantial litigation costs as a result.

If your spouse does not agree to your leaving the state, petition the court. If there is a valid reason for leaving, such as remarriage, an improved employment opportunity, or a health condition, and the removal is in the children's best interests, the court may grant permission to leave, with new arrangements made for visitation. Support arrangements can also be altered to accommodate the additional expense of transporting the children for visitation.

If the children are being taken out of the state to keep a parent from visiting or for some other reason not in the children's interest, the petition to remove may be denied. On the other hand, reduction of visitation time is generally not a sufficient basis for denying the petition to remove.

58. What if the custodian takes the children to live out of state without permission or court order?

A petition should be filed immediately in the court where the last custody order was entered, asking that the children be returned to their home state and that a contempt citation be issued against the parent who removed the children. A delay in filing this petition may suggest that you are indifferent or in agreement with the removal and will give the custodial parent an opportunity to establish a new home state for the children. The court will be reluctant to remove them from the new home if it has been established for six months or more without formal protest by the noncustodian.

Most state courts will allow the custodian to remove children from the state for good cause, and custody will not be changed solely because children have been removed without permission. If home-state orders to return the children are ignored, you will have to go to the state where the children are living to enforce your order. Disputes between state courts over the custody of children are common, but all states are now required to follow the jurisdictional guidelines of the Uniform Child Custody Jurisdiction Act.

59. What if the noncustodial parent takes the children to live out of state without permission?

If the children are not promptly returned, and you are unable to go to where they are living and bring them back, file an *immediate* petition for contempt of court. Your spouse has "snatched" the children and is subject to fine or imprisonment for a willful violation of the custody judgment.

If the contempt proceedings in your state are ignored by your spouse, you will have to go to the state where he or she is living to enforce your custody rights.

60. How are conflicts between state courts over the custody of children resolved?

Although the United States Constitution requires all states to give full faith and credit to the valid judgments of other states, this does not always happen in custody disputes. Because each state takes jurisdiction over the children within its borders, and because any custody judgments can be modified on proof of a substantial change of circumstances, custody issues are frequently, and unfortunately, relitigated as the children are moved from state to state.

To avoid these unsettling and expensive conflicts of laws, most states have enacted some form of the Uniform Child Custody Jurisdiction Act, which is designed to resolve interstate custody jurisdiction. The act sets forth rules to determine which state should properly have jurisdiction to decide a custody dispute and provides rules for the transfer of witnesses, social service investigative reports, and other evidence between state courts. By promoting cooperation among state courts, the act should curtail the gamesmanship between warring parents who move from state to state to seek favorable custodial decisions or to avoid the orders of a prior home state. Once states to which children are brought refuse to relitigate custody disputes and order children returned to their home state, the child-snatching epidemic we are now seeing should be eliminated.

The federal Parental Kidnapping Prevention Act, which became effective in 1981, requires that all state courts follow the jurisdictional standards of the Uniform Child Custody Jurisdiction Act. The federal law also makes available a parent locator service to track down kidnapping parents. The act directs the Justice Department to assist in the apprehension of parents if they violated state felony laws in removing a child to another state.

61. How are child custody disputes resolved when the parents live in different countries?

A parent can go to the country where the child is residing to litigate custody issues, but foreign courts have their own laws and procedures, which may vary drastically from our own. Treaties and conventions between nations define the terms under which nations will honor and enforce each other's custody judgments. Consult an attorney to determine whether such a treaty or convention on child custody exists between the countries involved in your case.

62. What can I do if my child has been abducted to a foreign country?

The United States is a signatory to the Hague Convention on child abduction, which establishes legal rights and procedures for the prompt return of children who have been wrongfully removed or retained abroad. The convention is honored by forty-nine countries, including most of Europe and the English-speaking countries. Like the Uniform Child Custody Jurisdiction Act and the Parental Kidnapping Prevention Act, which deal with abductions within the United States, the Hague Convention is a giant step toward reducing international child snatching.

CHAPTER VI

Child Support
and Visitation

63. How is the amount of child support determined?

Under pressure from the federal government, each state has enacted presumptive guidelines for child support based on a percentage of the supporting parent's net income. (See page 173 for sample Child Support Guidelines for California, Illinois, and New York.) "Net income" is usually defined as gross income from all sources less income and Social Security taxes, mandatory pension contributions, union dues, health insurance premiums, and necessary expenditures for the production of income. The court can order more or less support than called for in the guidelines where good cause is shown. For example, proof of special needs for the children will result in a higher percentage of income. Where one or both parents have such high incomes that guideline percentages exceed reasonable lifestyle needs of the children, a lower percentage may be ordered. Once the percentage of income is calculated, the support order will generally be stated in a fixed dollar amount. Otherwise, it would be difficult to know if the payor is in arrears.

64. Will my child support payments cover my total financial obligation to the children?

In addition to child support payments, the children are also entitled to ask for college expenses and extraordinary medical, dental, and hospitalization payments, life insurance, health insurance, and, in some states, support after the death of the supporting parent in the form of a probate estate claim.

The financially obligated parent is usually required to maintain health insurance for the children when it is available at a place of employment and some amount of life insurance geared to the children's standard of living and the number of years until they come of age.

The college expense requirement is usually limited to four years of undergraduate education or similar trade school training after high school. The amount the noncustodial parent usually has to contribute takes into consideration the financial means of both parents as well as any assets of the children.

In some states the duty to support children is not terminated upon death, and the custodial parent may make a claim in the divorce court for support from the estate of a deceased parent, either in periodic payments or in a lump sum.

Even if your decree doesn't provide for any of this extra child support, you are entitled to apply to the court for such support when the need arises.

65. Which parent can claim the dependent tax deduction for a child?

When parents are divorced or separated, the custodial parent can claim a dependent child exemption or execute IRS Form 8332 releasing the exemption to the noncustodial parent (see page 214). To qualify for the exemption the child must be in the custody of either or both parents for more than half of the calendar year and the parents must contribute over half the child's support. If there is no court decree or written separation agreement, the custodial parent can claim the exemption if the parents lived separately for the last six months or more of a calendar year. A divorced or separated parent cannot claim the dependency exemption unless both parents would have been entitled to the exemption had they been married and filed a joint return.

The noncustodial parent may claim the dependency deduction when the custodial parent transfers the deduction by a written declaration, if a multiple support agreement is in effect, or if the divorce or separation agreement was executed before 1985. The multiple support agreement exception applies if the child is supported collectively by a group of people who relinquish their right to claim the deduction.

66. Can I get child custody and support even though we are not divorced and there is no divorce suit pending?

Most states allow the filing of an action for custody and support of children, or for visitation, without the necessity of filing for divorce or legal separation. Every state has jurisdiction over the children within its borders, even if there is not a specific statute for custody or visitation or support suits. Where there is no pending action or judgment already entered in connection with custody or visitation, both parents have equal rights to have the children reside with them.

67. If a spouse remarries, is the new spouse's income taken into account when determining child support?

Technically, no. The new spouse has no obligation to support someone else's children. As a practical matter, however, the fact that a new spouse may be paying a lot of the household expenses is relevant in determining how much the noncustodial parent has available for support payments or how much the custodian needs for the children. For example, if the custodian mother was paying $500 monthly rent until she remarried and moved into her new husband's home rent-free, this is a relevant *need* consideration. Similarly, if a new wife applies her income to household expenses, her husband's *ability* to pay child support increases. Generally speaking, though, courts will not increase or decrease child support based solely on the income of the new spouse.

68. Can I get child support if my ex-spouse dies?

Yes, in the form of either a fixed dollar amount or a percentage of the estate. The more common arrangement, however, is to specify a life insurance obligation payable to the children. The payment in the event of death is quicker, simpler, and more certain. Support and alimony claims in the event of death can also be drafted as part of an estate plan that will reduce death taxes. In states which have adopted some form of the Uniform Marriage and Divorce Act, claims for continuing child support can be filed *after* the death of a supporting parent.

69. Must I pay support if my spouse is not allowing visitation, or must I allow visitation if my spouse is not paying support?

Yes, you must, unless a court order has been entered modifying your visitation or support obligation. The right of visitation and the duty to pay support are completely separate, and the court will enforce both independently. Some states have statutes, however, that allow the suspension of support if the custodial parent is willfully interfering with visitation rights. The suspension cannot be made unilaterally, as a court hearing must first be conducted to see if the visitation abuse is willful. In any case, a petition for contempt should be filed promptly with the court if support or visitation provisions are regularly violated.

In keeping with the separation of questions of support and visitation, it is also important not to pay support or discuss money in connection with picking up the children for visitation or returning them. The children undergo enough stress when a marital breakdown occurs and should not have visitation associated with money problems.

70. How are orders for visitation and support enforced?

You must file a petition for enforcement or similar proceeding in the court where your divorce is pending or where the divorce decree was entered.

All states now provide for support enforcement at no charge through the Friend of the Court or state's attorney. These programs usually involve support payments directly to the court clerk, who records and distributes them to the recipient. The transactions are computerized, and arrearage notices and enforcement proceedings are often automatic.

Another development in support enforcement is the automatic wage assignment. Recent legislation requires that all supporting parents execute a wage assignment at the time the support order is entered. The wage assignment automatically goes into effect if the supporting parent falls thirty or sixty days in arrears on the support payments. Thereafter, the current support and arrearages are automatically deducted from the supporting parent's wages until the arrearage is made up or until further order of the court.

An increasing number of support deadbeats is a national problem, and a serious effort is being made by state legislatures and governmental agencies to provide more aggressive child support enforcement at the state's expense.

71. Can I enforce my child support order in another state?

Yes. Remedies are available to enforce a child support arrearage in whatever state or U.S. territory the delinquent parent may be found. When parents live in different states, fixing, modifying, and enforcing child support orders is governed by the Uniform Interstate Family Support Act. Federal legislation requires that all states adopt this act by January 1998. Government child support agencies and private attorneys both can pursue child support claims in another state under this act without the necessity of traveling to the other state. Legal services provided by the support agencies are free of charge. Application can be made for contribution from the other spouse for fees and costs if you use a private attorney.

One of the principal advantages of the Uniform Act is that it assures that there will be only one child support order in effect rather than conflicting orders from different states. Either parent can apply for support modifications under the act if there has been a material change in circumstances since the last order was entered. Since it is now a federal crime to cross state lines for the purpose of avoiding support obligations, the federal government will also assist in tracking down delinquent parents through the Parent Locator Service of the U.S. Attorney's Office.

72. What is reasonable visitation?

Reasonable visitation describes a noncustodial parent's visiting rights when specific times are not detailed in the agreement or decree. The term implies a mutual understanding as to expected periods of visitation and will, therefore, vary. Note the sample visitation provisions on page 43 to compare very light visitation with very extensive visitation schedules. Any combination of these paragraphs can be used to tailor your visitation provisions if what the parent considers "reasonable" is not satisfactory.

CAUTION: If you and your spouse cannot agree on what is "reasonable," then it is definitely recommended that you have the specific periods of visitation spelled out in the decree.

73. Can people other than parents sue for visitation rights?

The current trend has been to allow grandparents, great-grandparents, and even siblings to petition for visitation rights with minor children when special circumstances or the best interests of the children make such contact appropriate. State laws vary on nonparent visitation rights, so you will have to consult your attorney. Nonparent visitation is not guaranteed and may be substantially less than what is normal for parents.

74. When should the children meet the new girl- or boyfriend?

Take your time. If you're still married and your spouse is likely to be hostile to "exposing" the children to your friend, then save them from the additional pressure of dealing with your new relationship. The children will generally reflect the attitude of your spouse toward marital "rivals." Let them adjust to the reality of your divorce before forcing a meeting with someone they may resent out of jealousy or loyalty to their other parent. When the children *want* to meet your friend you'll know it, and that's the best time. In the meanwhile, resist the temptation to involve the children in this new relationship, which may, in fact, be only temporary.

75. What can be done about the child who refuses to visit?

Not much. Hostility between parents is often behind the child's reluctance. Forcing the child, either by parental pressure or by court orders, only intensifies the problem. Even if the custodial parent is the proven culprit in discouraging visitation, the child will probably resent the imposition of court sanctions. Patience and psychological counseling are the only hope for altering the child's attitude. It is not uncommon for the child to outgrow this kind of reluctance and even to reject the parent who was encouraging it.

76. Can children have their own lawyers?

Yes. Sometimes parents and their lawyers lose sight of children's best interest in their zeal to "win." Where that is the case, or if the children are mistreated in any way, the children should have their own attorney.

VISITATION PROVISIONS—SAMPLE

Light visitation schedule

The father/mother shall have the right to visit* with the minor children on alternate Saturdays and Sundays, on alternate national holidays, and for an extended period during the children's summer vacation.

Average visitation schedule

The father/mother shall visit with the minor children on alternate weekends from Saturday at (10:00 A.M.) until Sunday at (7:00 P.M.) and one evening per week for dinner. In addition, the father/mother shall visit on alternate national and religious holidays, to wit: Christmas Day, New Year's Day, Easter Sunday, Memorial Day, Fourth of July, Labor Day, and Thanksgiving. The holiday visitation shall be from 9:00 A.M. to 8:00 P.M. When the holiday occurs on a Monday, the children shall be with the father/mother the preceding weekend, notwithstanding the provision for alternate weekend visitation. In addition, the father/mother shall have visitation for one half the Christmas vacation, alternate spring vacations, and for four weeks during the children's summer vacation.

Extraordinary visitation

The father/mother shall have visitation with the children every weekend from Friday after school until Sunday evening; on alternate national and religious holidays (see above) for one half of the Christmas vacation; for all of the spring vacation, and for six weeks during the summer. The father/mother shall also have the right to take the children out to dinner two nights per week and to contact them at least once per day by telephone.

* This does *not* mean visit in the custodial parent's home. In most cases visits are specifically *not* in that home.

In an increasing number of states, it is the regular practice to appoint a guardian or a lawyer to represent the children's interests in custody litigation. The guardian-lawyer usually conducts an investigation into the children's home environment and explores particular issues raised by the parents in the custody or visitation dispute. The lawyer then reports back either to the court or to the lawyers for the parties and sometimes makes a recommendation as to the best temporary or permanent arrangement for the children.

The weight given to this recommendation by the court is generally substantial. The guardian has a great deal of influence in determining who is given custody because he or she is considered to be impartial and is concerned only with the best interests of the clients, the children. The impartial opinion of the children's representative, after a thorough investigation, often results in a custody settlement without trial, since both lawyers understand that the court is most likely to follow his or her recommendations. Face-saving compromises are reached, and a lot of expense and acrimony is avoided. *Representing Children: Standards for Attorneys and Guardians,* published by the American Academy of Matrimonial Lawyers, discusses the responsibilities of the children's legal representative. A copy can be obtained by contacting the academy office at (312) 263-6477.

77. What may be involved in the guardian–lawyer's investigation and representation of the children?

Interviewing the children

Interviewing parents or potential custodians

Interviewing teachers, neighbors, and other knowledgeable third parties

Investigating the home and neighborhood

Examining school and medical records

Suggesting psychological evaluations or treatment for children or their parents

Conducting or attending depositions

Filing motions on behalf of the children regarding visitation, abuse, health or other problems that the parents haven't called to the attention of the court or been able to resolve themselves

Filing a report of the investigation (optional)

Attending court during trial and preliminary motions

Making recommendations (optional) to the court or counsels for the parents on a variety of matters dealing with the children, including custody and visitation

Protecting the children's financial interest in connection with support, health and educational expenses, and seeking a portion of the parents' estate in the event of death or as security for support payments

78. Who pays the guardian–lawyer's fees and costs?

Either or both parents, depending on their respective financial ability. Children's assets can also be applied to the cost of their representation.

CHAPTER VII

Alimony and Property Division

79. How do I know if I'm entitled to alimony?

Alimony, sometimes called "maintenance," is spousal support and is not awarded in every case. In general, alimony is awarded to spouses who need it from spouses who can afford to pay it. Divorce reform legislation of the 1960s and '70s favored property awards over alimony to reduce postdivorce financial dependence. Rehabilitative alimony for a limited term to give divorced spouses time to retrain or to establish careers was the support concept of the no-fault revolution. Unfortunately, cultural and economic realities left little opportunity for most women to support themselves at the living standard they enjoyed during their marriage. In many states the legislative pendulum is swinging back to a more favorable alimony climate. While financial need and the other spouse's ability to meet that need after divorce is still the legal cornerstone for alimony, reimbursement for career contributions is another factor that many states recognize. The wife who works while her husband attends college or graduate school is now more likely to share in the fruits of that education after divorce by sharing the income it produces through alimony. Your attorney will have to determine if you qualify for alimony under your state laws and for how long. Some states still have no court-ordered alimony, and others limit it to short-term rehabilitation or to spouses who are mentally or physically incapacitated.

80. Are there different kinds of alimony?

Yes. While the terminology varies, you generally have *periodic alimony* for an indefinite period, *alimony in gross* in a lump sum or for a fixed period, and *reviewable alimony* for a fixed period with the right to continue or modify it, depending on future financial circumstances. Rehabilitative alimony generally falls in the last category. The right to periodic and reviewable alimony generally terminates upon the death of either spouse or the remarriage of the recipient. By written agreement any combination of the alimony types can be created to meet the anticipated or uncertain needs of spouses. In any case, you want to know if the alimony is going to be modifiable by the court, if it will be terminable upon certain future events, and if it is taxable to the recipient.

81. How is the amount of alimony determined?

In most cases the amount of periodic alimony payments is based on the anticipated financial need of the recipient spouse after the divorce and the ability of the paying spouse to support that need from income, property, or both. The level of need is based on the cost of maintaining the lifestyle the spouses established during the marriage. Ability to pay takes into account the right of the paying spouse to maintain a similar lifestyle. Unfortunately, only the wealthy can sustain their married standard of living after divorce without another income being added to the mix. That is why so many women have to rejoin the workforce after a divorce in low- to upper-middle-income families.

While the legal duty to pay alimony is gender neutral, the incidence of wives paying alimony is comparatively small. If the wife has sufficient income or property to support herself, there will be no alimony unless the purpose is to compensate her for contributions to her husband's career or somehow to balance the property division. Most settlements include a combination of property division and alimony payments, which take advantage of the tax deductibility of alimony to benefit both spouses.

82. What if there is not enough money to support two families?

This is true in the majority of marital separations. The separated families often have to live at a lower standard than when they lived together because basic living costs are doubled. There may be increased pressure because a spouse who worked two or more jobs or regularly did overtime work frequently will drop extra work to avoid having the added income computed as a factor in any support order. The money crunch is normally tightest during the divorce, when new costs are being encountered and income is being strategically suppressed. Part of the strategy may be to force an unemployed spouse to get a job, and in many cases employment of both spouses is a necessity.

83. How long is alimony paid?

There are no hard-and-fast rules, though it is unusual to pay alimony for more years than the marriage lasted. Periodic alimony is paid until the death of either spouse or the remarriage of the recipient. Rehabilitative alimony is generally in the three- to five-year range, subject to possible renewal. Alimony in gross is paid over whatever period the parties agree, from a single lump sum to monthly payments for many years. By agreement the parties can fix their own termination provisions.

84. Will cohabiting after the divorce affect my alimony payments?

Yes, in most states continued sharing of a residence with a person of the opposite sex will be treated like a remarriage if the alimony payments are periodic and subject to termination. Unlike a remarriage, which automatically terminates periodic alimony, residential cohabitation is a question of fact, which must be proved in a court hearing. Short-term cohabitation may not result in alimony termination.

85. Am I better off settling for property instead of alimony?

That depends on a number of factors, including the value of property compared with the amount of alimony you might have received. Generally, a husband prefers to pay alimony over time rather than an equal value in property transferred right now. The alimony can be tax deductible and the obligation may end early because of death or remarriage. If the husband is a bad risk in terms of future payments, the wife may be willing to discount the total alimony stream for the security of a lump sum in cash or property now with no tax to pay. Before making this often difficult decision, you should compute the present dollar value of the alimony right that you are exchanging for cash or other property, taking taxes, remarriage potential, and the satisfaction of finality into account. Your lawyer's help in assessing the options is particularly important.

86. Are alimony payments taxable?

Yes. Alimony is deductible by the payor spouse and taxable to the recipient spouse, but only if all the requirements of federal income tax laws have been satisfied:

1. The obligation to pay alimony must arise from a written divorce or separation instrument that includes a court decree of divorce or separation, a court order of spousal support, or a written separation agreement entered into by the spouses. Oral agreements or support letters written by attorneys that are not signed by the parties do not qualify for alimony deduction purposes. Neither do payments that predate a written instrument.

2. The alimony payments must be by cash or check, as opposed to rendering of services or transfer or use of property.

3. The payment must be made to the other spouse or to a third party on behalf of the other spouse, such as payment of the spouse's living expenses or insurance premiums. The written instrument must provide for third-party payments on behalf of a spouse for them to qualify as deductible alimony.

4. The obligation to continue alimony payments must terminate upon the death of the recipient spouse. It is not necessary that the payments terminate upon the recipient spouse's remarriage or the payor's death.

5. The spouses must not occupy the same household when the alimony payments are made unless they are separated by a voluntary separation agreement or support decree.

6. Payments under the instrument in the first separation year cannot exceed the average payments in years 2 and 3 by more than $15,000 per year. Otherwise, the excess is not tax deductible.

7. Payments specifically designated as child support or property division in the written instrument are not deductible or taxable as alimony.

8. Child support payments combined with the alimony without allocation are deductible in their entirety. However, any portion of the unallocated payment that can be identified or fixed as child support under the terms of the agreement will not be deductible or taxable.

9. Payments that would otherwise qualify as alimony are not deductible or taxable if the spouses so agree in their written divorce or separation instrument. This can be an important concession in any settlement negotiation. If your attorney is not familiar with the tax laws as they relate to divorce and separation, an accountant should review your final agreement or court decree to make sure the intended after-tax effect of support payments has been properly drafted. This is an area for creative tax planning to get the most after-tax mileage out of available family support dollars. A judge who is called upon to decide support issues is not likely to be nearly as creative as tax-conscious attorneys.

87. Will I lose my spouse's group health insurance after the divorce?

Not if your final decree includes a COBRA provision allowing you to continue your spouse's group health coverage for three years following the divorce. States also have laws mandating extended health coverage for nonemployee spouses after a divorce. While all of these federal and state laws have time limitations for the continued coverage, an insurance adviser should be able to find you substitute permanent coverage before your time limit runs out. If you have preexisting health problems, start looking for your substitute coverage *now*.

88. Will our children be covered by group health insurance after a divorce?

Normally a spouse with group health insurance will be required to insure your children after a divorce. Federal legislation also provides for mandatory medical coverage for children under group health insurance plans. Any child of a health plan participant is covered if the child is identified in a judgment, decree, or order entered under a state domestic relations law providing for child support or health benefit coverage. A Qualified Medical Child Support Order (QMCSO) must identify the child and the plan and must describe the type of coverage and period that it applies. The order cannot require the insurer to provide benefits not already in the plan. See a sample QMCSO on page 208.

89. Will I remain the beneficiary of my spouse's life insurance after the divorce?

That depends on the terms of your settlement or court decree. Life insurance is a valuable security device to assure compliance with a provision for future support or a property settlement in periodic payments. Since the owner of an insurance policy can change the beneficiary at any time, it is important to negotiate life insurance protection and include the specifics in the final decree. A copy of the decree should then be sent to the insurance company with a request for confirmation that the company will comply with the judgment. Any divorce involving minor children should also include insurance protection on the life of the supporting parent or on the lives of both parents. Absent an agreement, courts may refuse to order life insurance protection for spouses if the duty to pay support terminates on the death of the payor.

90. What property is divided in a divorce case?

The divorce court has jurisdiction over all property in which either spouse or their children have an interest. Therefore, a complete divorce makes a provision for all property subject to the property division laws of your state. All states operate under an *equitable distribution* or a *community property* system or some combination of the two. Under both systems, a spouse's *separate* or *nonmarital* property acquired before the marriage or during the marriage by gift or inheritance is awarded to that spouse. The balance of property acquired by either spouse during the marriage is presumed to be *marital* or *community* property, subject to division between the spouses. Whether particular property is classified as marital or nonmarital can be the subject of extensive discovery to trace the origins of assets that were purchased or exchanged from a nonmarital source. State laws vary on the fine points of nonmarital tracing and the effect of value increase resulting from marital or nonmarital contributions. You will have to consult your lawyer on this complex and ever-changing facet of divorce law.

91. How is property classified as marital or nonmarital?

The basic concept in both community property and equitable distribution states is that marriage is a partnership, and all income earned and property acquired during the marriage is marital (equitable division term) or community (community property term). Marital/community property is subject to division between the spouses regardless of which spouse holds title. Nonmarital or separate property as it's called in some states was owned by one spouse before marriage or acquired by one spouse during the marriage by gift or inheritance. Parties may also agree that certain property is nonmarital. State laws differ as to whether the appreciation and income from nonmarital property remains nonmarital and what effect the spouses' marital and nonmarital contributions have on property classification. Tracing existing property to its nonmarital source can be a factual and legal quagmire requiring extensive discovery and proof to rebut the legal presumption that any property acquired during the marriage is marital. In any case, once an asset or liability has been classified as separate property, it must be awarded to the owner spouse.

92. How is community property divided?

Three of the community property states (California, Louisiana, and New Mexico) divide community property equally between the spouses in terms of value if not in kind. The other five (Arizona, Idaho, Nevada, Texas, and Washington) divide community property as it would be divided in an equitable distribution state.

93. How is property divided in equitable distribution states?

The judge is given discretion to distribute the property based on various factors, including respective financial and homemaker contributions, duration of the marriage, current and potential financial condition of the parties, and dissipation or waste of marital assets.

There is no presumption of equal division, and homemaker contributions are generally given equal weight with financial contributions.

94. Who pays family debts in a divorce?

Debts are classified as marital and nonmarital just as assets are. Non-marital debts generally arise in connection with the acquisition or maintenance of nonmarital assets and are assigned to the owning spouse. Marital debts are divided as part of the marital estate. Personal debts, like charge accounts, are generally assigned to the party who incurred them, and other marital debts are generally assigned to the spouse best able to pay them. The assigned liability is then set off against that spouse's marital property award to compute his or her net marital award. The equity or fairness of a property division is measured by comparing the net marital estates awarded to each spouse.

95. What if a spouse fails to comply with a court order to pay a debt?

Most judgments have indemnification clauses in connection with debt assignments. If a spouse fails to pay the debt, the creditor can sue both spouses in a collection suit, but the divorce court will enforce the indemnification against the defaulting spouse. The indemnification requires a reimbursement to the innocent spouse for any loss or expense arising from the creditor's suit, including attorneys' fees. The likelihood of these creditor suits is substantially reduced if the debts are identified in the decree and payment is made from a specified source as soon as the divorce decree is entered.

96. Will my spouse's retirement benefits be divided as part of a divorce proceeding?

Yes, and so will yours. Any retirement benefit accrued during the marriage is subject to division upon divorce. This includes pensions, profit sharing, individual retirement accounts, or any work-related benefit payable upon or after retirement. Premarital retirement benefits will first be separated from the marital portion by a formula used in your state and assigned to the owner spouse as separate property. The balance will either be valued and set off against other marital property awarded in the case or be divided in kind by a Qualified Domestic Relations Order, or QDRO.

CAUTION: Typically, income taxes are not assessed against retirement benefits when they are acquired but are deferred until the benefits are actually distributed. While the deferral can continue beyond your divorce, it is important to understand your tax obligations arising from any division of retirement benefits.

97. When are retirement benefits divided between spouses?

The division will occur as soon as the necessary paperwork is completed following entry of your divorce decree, but your right to spend the money may be deferred until you are 59½ years old. The Employee Retirement Income Security Act (ERISA) allows divorcing spouses to divide retirement plans pursuant to a judgment, decree, or order entered in accordance with a state domestic relations law. The operative document with tax-qualified plans is the Qualified Domestic Relations Order, which can assign all or a portion of the benefits payable to a participant spouse to the divorced spouse (alternate payee). Individual retirement accounts and nonqualified plans can be transferred as part of a divorce as well, but the formalities of a QDRO are not required. Note that the transferred retirement benefits will have to be held in the alternate payee's IRA or tax-qualified retirement plan until age 59½. A 20 percent tax withholding is required unless the transfer is directly to the plan or IRA. Your attorney or tax adviser should be consulted in any case, because this complex area of tax law is frequently revised, and careful planning is necessary to avoid penalties from early or unauthorized benefit withdrawals. A sample QDRO can be found on page 206.

98. Are property transfers in a divorce taxable?

A transfer of property to you or your spouse as part of a divorce is not taxable at the time of transfer, but it is subject to capital gains taxes at the time you sell it. The capital gain is computed on the increase in value of the asset from the time of its original purchase. That original *cost basis* is passed through to the recipient spouse when the divorce is finalized. It is essential, therefore, that you receive all records reflecting the cost basis of property transferred to you in your divorce so you can calculate any capital gain or loss when you sell it. Transfers between divorced spouses are not taxable at the time of transfer if made within one year of the divorce or within six years of the divorce if the transfer is pursuant to the divorce or separation instrument.

99. Is our marital residence given special tax treatment?

Yes. Special tax code provisions allowing deferral and limited exclusions of capital gains on residential home sales have been replaced and dramatically broadened by 1997 tax legislation. The new legislation provides that for home sales after May 6, 1997, married taxpayers may exclude up to $500,000 in capital gains if: (a) they file a joint tax return in the year of sale (divorced spouses may not file a joint income tax return); (b) one of the spouses owned the property for at least two of the previous five years; (c) both spouses used the home as a principal residence for at least two of the previous five years; (d) neither spouse had a previous sale of a principal residence where there was a capital gain exclusion within the previous two years.

If the spouses are divorced in the year of their home sale, then each of them can exclude up to $250,000 in gain if the other conditions are met. Consult your accountant to make sure you qualify for this substantial tax savings. You may also wish to coordinate the timing of the entry of your divorce decree and sale of your home to qualify for the joint income tax filing status.

100. How do I keep track of assets and liabilities as my case progresses?

The most valuable tool to keep track of your case during discovery, negotiation, and trial is a Comparative Balance Sheet. A sample is included on page 186. There is a "value" column for both husband and wife, so you can list each property with your opinion of value and with your spouse's. When the values are the same or close you do not need appraisals. Larger differences can sometimes be compromised or given to your spouse if you believe your spouse's value is inflated. You may want to keep assets your spouse has undervalued. The Comparative Balance Sheet encourages this kind of horse trading and provides a convenient checklist so you do not overlook assets or liabilities in the heat of a negotiation or trial. Judges also appreciate a Comparative Balance Sheet because it reduces even a complicated case to a convenient nutshell for settlement discussions or trial.

101. Should we file a joint tax return?

In most cases the answer is yes, if a joint return saves you both money. A joint return *cannot* be filed for the year in which you are divorced, but often there is an overlap, and part of a settlement agreement will involve tax returns and division of tax refunds or liability. If an arbitrary refusal to sign a joint return results in a substantial financial loss, that loss will usually be reflected in some other aspect of the settlement by a disproportionate division of property or an increase or reduction of support. Your attorney will encourage you to file a joint return if doing so is to your mutual benefit.

If your taxable income comes primarily from your spouse and you fear the information provided the Internal Revenue Service will not be legitimate, insist on a written indemnification from your spouse for liability for additional taxes or penalties. Even if you did not prepare the return or make misrepresentations regarding your personal income or deductions, Internal Revenue will seek collection from both of you, but the indemnification will entitle you to reimbursement from your spouse for any loss.

CONSIDER: If the difference between a joint and a separate return is substantial, the willingness to file jointly can be an important leverage factor in settlement negotiations.

CHAPTER VIII

Financial Hide-and-Seek
with Your Spouse

102. What do I do first to protect myself financially?

If you haven't already done so for the preliminary interview, start gathering information regarding income and assets so that you and your lawyer can budget projected needs for yourself and other members of the family. This effort becomes part of what is called the "discovery procedure." (See also Chapter XI, Discovery Procedures.)

1. First determine what property you own, when it was acquired and how, its value, and how title is held. (The Asset/Liability Worksheet on page 216 will assist you.)

2. Determine the actual physical whereabouts of assets and title documents. If you own stock, note where the certificates are kept, and where the passbooks for savings accounts are, as well as deeds and other records regarding real estate, etc.

3. If property is missing, or you suspect your spouse may have acquired property without your knowledge, make note of these facts and call them to your lawyer's attention. (Hiding assets and suffering convenient memory lapses are common behavior for otherwise honest spouses when a divorce is imminent. Review the Hidden Asset Checklist on page 67 to assist you in your search.)

Once you know the nature and extent of your assets, and their physical location, you and your lawyer are in a much better position to obtain a fair property division and support agreement.

CAUTION: Discuss with your lawyer what original documents such as bearer bonds, canceled checks, or savings account passbooks you should hold in safekeeping. Find out if some documents should be copied and replaced without the knowledge of your spouse. If they are later hidden, altered, or disappear, you can use that dishonesty as a leverage factor to your own advantage.

103. Should I close bank accounts?

This is a legitimate act of self-protection if you are able and willing to account for the withdrawn money. If you dissipate it or cannot prove how you spent it, you may delay the settlement of your case and encourage countergamesmanship by your spouse.

CAUTION: What starts out as an act of self-protection may escalate into a full-scale war of hide-and-seek. Store your grandmother's silver flatware in your friend's attic if you feel you must, but be prepared to account for its whereabouts, and don't be surprised if the antique clock disappears from the mantel.

104. What should I do about safe-deposit boxes?

If the boxes are joint, at least inventory the contents. If self-protection requires safekeeping until injunctive protection has been obtained, place the contents in another box or some other safe place. In any event, have a neutral third party present when you inventory the box, because you can expect your spouse to claim that your accounting of the contents was not complete. The neutral third party can initial your inventory and verify its accuracy at a later date. A bank employee will be more credible than a friend or relative as your witness.

105. What will the court do if I hide marital assets?

If you act affirmatively to hide assets or knowingly fail to disclose assets, you are committing a fraud and could be held in contempt of court. If the hidden asset is discovered even after the divorce, you are subject to a fine and the asset may be awarded to your spouse. Unfortunately, the breakdown in mutual trust that is common to failed marriages causes most spouses to suspect their partners are hiding assets. Until that suspicion is alleviated, it is very difficult to settle cases. In the meantime, substantial expense and delay will result from the search for hidden assets, which may be unwarranted. If you want your divorce to be expedited with minimum acrimony, encourage trust with voluntary and full asset disclosure from the outset. If your lawyer tolerates any scheme to hide assets or withhold pertinent information, you've got a bad lawyer and should look elsewhere.

It is one thing to hide assets and not admit they exist. It is quite another merely to put the assets in safekeeping or use them for necessaries. For example, if you remove funds from a joint bank account and hold them in your own name, or place joint stock certificates in your own safe-deposit box, there is no problem as long as you admit their existence. The judge will not be concerned if the assets are available for division and distribution. On the other hand, if you claim you lost the money from a joint account at the racetrack, the judge may assume you are lying even if you are not. If you hide or dissipate marital assets, the judge may award you the *missing* assets and award an equal amount of the remaining assets to your spouse.

106. What is dissipation of assets?

A review of your spouse's canceled checks and credit card statements is the best way to discover and document dissipation of marital assets. Expenditures for activities and items that do not favor common marital interests during a period of marital breakdown are presumed to be dissipation and are subject to reimbursement by the dissipating spouse. Post the suspected examples of dissipation to your spreadsheet of hidden assets and the burden will shift to your spouse to explain the marital purpose of each expenditure. Travel and entertainment with friends of the opposite sex, gifts for nonfamily members, gambling losses, living expenses in a separate home after a spouse leaves the marital residence, and payment of attorney fees have all been held to be dissipation. Once the extent of dissipation has been quantified, the most common remedy is to add that sum back to the marital estate and award it to the dissipating spouse as if it still existed. Expenditures for nonmarital purposes that occur before or after a period of marital breakdown are not classified as dissipation. Definition of the "period of marital breakdown" varies in different states. The trend has been to restrict this period because cases are complicated and prolonged by angry spouses demanding discovery back many years. Some courts even restrict dissipation claims to the period when the divorce suit is pending.

If you can prove that certain assets were spent for a marital purpose, such as the payment of family debts or legitimate living expenses, there will probably be no penalty, unless the expenditure was in violation of a court restraining order.

CAUTION: Men or women who are the principal source of family income should consider satisfying outstanding debts from family assets *before* restraining orders are entered. Since you will probably have to pay these debts anyhow, you might as well get contribution from your spouse by using marital assets before the marital estate is divided.

107. What should I do about charge accounts?

Since both spouses are legally liable for balances due on joint charge accounts, your decision to close them depends on how much you *trust* your spouse. If he or she has a history of financial irresponsibility, or if there is a likelihood of vindictiveness, you should probably terminate these accounts. If you have no such fear, leave joint accounts in status quo to avoid recriminations for what your spouse may consider an aggressive or threatening act.

108. Will I be liable for my spouse's charges?

You are liable for family debts if you actually contracted for the debts, or if the law of your state holds *both* spouses liable for the legitimate family expenses of *either*. For example, if you have signed up for a credit card such as MasterCard or Visa, and if your spouse is an authorized signatory on the account, then you both will be liable for any charges as a matter of contract obligation. If your spouse is charging necessities such as food and clothing, even if it is with merchants with whom you have never dealt, you may still be jointly liable under family expense laws. These laws vary from state to state, and a lawyer should be consulted to see, for example, whether you can be held liable for the mink coat your wife has charged or the expensive boat your husband has contracted to buy—as distinct from clothing for the children. In some states it is a defense to such charges that you are living separate and apart without your fault. In most cases these accounts will have to be settled as part of an overall settlement or court adjudication.

The disposition of these bills could be a key stumbling block in resolving a case. As a general rule, if charges are made out of necessity and not in violation of a court injunction, the supporting spouse will pay them. But if charges are made for unnecessary items or out of vindictiveness, the other spouse may refuse to pay them, and final settlement is stymied until someone agrees to assume liability.

If outstanding bills are not settled in the divorce case, then creditors will sue either or both spouses in separate creditor suits. A creditor can sue you even if your spouse was ordered to pay the bill in the divorce case. If that happens, you must file a petition in the divorce case to have the debtor spouse defend you in the creditor suit and pay any judgment or related costs.

109. Should I establish my own credit?

Yes. It is wise to do this under any circumstances. Although creditors may be willing to add an unemployed spouse to a credit account while the parties are living together as husband and wife, the unemployed spouse may have difficulty when a separation or divorce is discovered. In spite of recent federal credit legislation, most creditors are still hesitant to extend credit to someone who has no visible means of support. Therefore, it makes sense *before any formal dissolution proceedings* to write a creditor and obtain cards in your individual name if you don't already have them. See the Credit Guide on page 64 for information on applying for credit.

110. How should I apply for credit if my spouse and I had accounts together?

First, be sure to list your *best* credit accounts. Tell the creditor about accounts you shared with your spouse. The creditor must consider this credit history when evaluating your application if you can show it applies to you. If the accounts are not on file at your local credit bureau, the creditor should call the previous creditors to verify the information you provided.

111. If the credit history from my marriage is bad, and I'm not responsible for it, what can I do?

Give a creditor information to show that this history should not be used against you. This would be true, for example, if a wife signed her husband's application for a card he used only for business. She never saw the bills and didn't know of the account's delinquent status. A creditor may take this into consideration when evaluating her application for an individual account.

On the other hand, if a department store account is in the name of one spouse but is used primarily by the other, and the account has been delinquent, this also needs to be called to the creditor's attention.

112. What do I do if I am denied credit?

Call the creditor and ask to speak with the credit manager—not a clerk. Make sure you ask the manager why you have been denied. Under the Equal Credit Opportunity Act (ECOA), you have the right to know the specific reasons your application was denied. If you ask to see your file within thirty days after you are notified that your credit application was denied, the bureau cannot charge you a fee for disclosure.

Next, check the report for accuracy and act on any misrepresentations. Then try to give the creditor any additional information that will show you are a good credit risk.

Unfortunately, the financial irresponsibility of your spouse may have an adverse effect on your credit rating. Credit organizations in your area will pick up the poor payment records of either spouse and attribute them to both. The only way out of this problem is to ask particular retailers what credit services they are using and then apply to *each* service for correction of the records regarding you personally. While the appeal process may vary with each credit service, persistence in applying to a responsible officer with a detailed explanation of who was liable for the credit abuse should expunge the bad record.

113. What do we do about credit cards during and after divorce?

"During" refers to questions 107 and 108. At the end of a divorce the cards should be in the name of only one spouse to absolve the other of financial responsibility and to protect the continuing credit history of each card. If one spouse takes the card as part of the divorce settlement, the other spouse should inform the creditor that he or she is no longer responsible for that account.

For more information about your right to a separate credit history write:

Credit History
Division of Credit Practices
Federal Trade Commission
Washington, D.C. 20580
(202) 326-2222

See the Credit Guide on page 64.

114. How can I find hidden assets?

By meticulously checking and tracing facts surrounding the acquisition and disposition of marital assets. Your present knowledge and the Hidden Asset Checklist on page 67 will get you started. Discuss your search and your discoveries with your lawyer, but *not* with your spouse. The more information you can find without your spouse's knowing that you are looking, the less likelihood there is of covering up. Your spouse is more likely to be caught in lies or evasions if you keep what you have found out about hidden assets to yourself and your lawyer. Keep your cards to your breast is the rule where gamesmanship is in operation. (See Chapter XI for Discovery Procedures.)

CONSIDER: Don't confront your spouse with proven lies without leveraging that knowledge to your advantage in future negotiations or litigation. *Don't waste it on a self-righteous scene.*

115. What if property or debts are omitted from the divorce decree in an honest mistake?

The court retains jurisdiction to open the case to rectify honest mistakes if you act promptly to petition the court as soon as the mistake is discovered. Sometimes settlement agreements have a catchall clause for debts or assets discovered after the divorce. Such items may be divided between the parties by a formula provided in the agreement. Failure to act promptly when a mutual mistake is discovered or negligence in discovering the error may cause the court to refuse to act. In that case, you and your spouse will have to resolve the matter on your own. You can both be sued by creditors for forgotten debts.

116. What if a significant asset or income source is omitted from the divorce decree because it was hidden or someone lied?

That would amount to fraud, which is grounds for opening up final judgments if action is taken promptly after the fraud is discovered. As in the case of mutual mistake, court jurisdiction will be declined if you do not act promptly. What relief the court gives depends on the nature and extent of the fraudulent omission or misstatement. The judgment may be amended slightly to correct the defect or vacated altogether if the defect is substantial. The party who acted fraudulently may also be charged with the attorneys' fees and costs incurred to correct the decree.

117. Can someone file bankruptcy to avoid court-ordered support or property division?

As a general rule a bankruptcy will discharge property obligations but will not discharge child support or spousal maintenance obligations. Bankruptcy courts look at the substance of the obligation and not just the language of the decree to determine what is property or support. For example, a husband's obligation to pay the wife's attorneys' fees, to pay marital debts, or to convey the marital residence have been held to be in the nature of support and not dischargeable. You should notify your attorney promptly if your spouse files for bankruptcy. An appearance in the bankruptcy court may be necessary to protect your rights under your support order or decree.

CREDIT GUIDE

What is a credit history?
A record of your payments on credit cards, charge accounts, installment loans, and mortgages.

Why do I need a good credit history?
Many people, especially women, are denied credit each year because they can't prove they handled credit well before. A good credit history will assure future credit success.

How do creditors find out about my credit history?
They ask you questions about your credit accounts or references on their application forms. Creditors may also ask for reports from credit bureaus. These reports confirm the references you provide and give a full picture of your financial situation.

What is a credit bureau?
A company that gathers and sells credit information about consumers. The bureau sends the creditor whatever information is on file about you. It will report how many and what kinds of credit accounts you have, how you pay your bills, and whether you have ever filed for bankruptcy or been sued for payment.

Where does the credit bureau get its information?
Directly from the creditors. Only accounts that make *regular* reports to the bureaus will appear in the files. While most national credit card companies report their accounts to the bureau, many local creditors do not. In addition, some creditors report only delinquent accounts and fail to report accounts with good payment histories.

Suppose creditors didn't have or didn't furnish information on me?
Then the credit bureau will report that it has "no file" on you. "No file" reports can cause an application to be rejected.

What if all our credit accounts were listed under only my spouse's name?
You may have problems. Many women who had the responsibility of paying monthly bills on time discover after being widowed or divorced that their credit history is all in their husbands' names. Creditors requesting information on the wives may get "no file" reports from the credit bureau.

A woman who marries and changes her name can have the same problem. The old accounts held in her maiden name may not be transferred to the file listed under her married name and her credit history may get lost. When applying for credit, mention your maiden name if you used it fairly recently.

What do I do if I never had credit?

Start building a good record now. A local bank or a drugstore or department store will often approve your credit application even if you don't meet the standards of a national creditor. It is a way to begin, and these people will become your future references.

Can I apply for as many accounts as I want?

No. Don't apply for too many accounts at one time. Credit bureaus keep a record of each creditor who inquires about you. Some creditors will deny your application if they think that you are opening too many new accounts in a short period of time. *Remember:* Most creditors are in business to *grant* credit, not deny it.

What if I shared accounts with my spouse that were established before June 1, 1977, and now are closed?

Under the Equal Credit Opportunity Act the creditor must report information on shared accounts established *after* June 1, 1977, to bureaus in both spouses' names. However, for prior accounts, visit or phone your local credit bureau to check whether these accounts are in your file. They are still a part of your credit history even though they are closed. If these accounts were reported in only your husband's or former husband's name, ask to have them added to your file too. The credit bureau cannot charge you for placing information already reported under your husband's name into a file accessible under your name.

Even if the accounts aren't in your husband's file, ask the bureau to add them to your file. You may need to pay a fee for each item added.

How about accounts opened after June 1, 1977?

In such accounts, you must indicate on the application whether you want to share the account with your spouse. Again, the creditor must report information on shared accounts established after June 1, 1977, to credit bureaus in both spouses' names.

How can I have credit information on accounts opened before June 1, 1977, included in my file?

Fill out the following form (make copies for the number you will need) and send it to the creditor you wish to report your history to the bureau. This will be useful if particular applications are denied or ignored.

CREDIT HISTORY FOR MARRIED PERSONS

Send a copy of this form to your *creditors* to have credit history information on existing accounts opened *before* June 1, 1977, reported to credit bureaus in both spouses' names.

Under the Equal Credit Opportunity Act, I request that you report all credit information on this account in both our names.

_____
Account number

Name—Print or Type

_____
First   *Middle*   *Last*

_____
First   *Middle*   *Last*

_____
Street, Number, Apt.

_____
City, State, Zip

_____
Signature of either spouse

HIDDEN ASSET CHECKLIST

In the course of discovery, most spouses believe that their counterparts have somehow hidden or failed to disclose the existence of certain assets. (See Chapter XI, Discovery Procedures.) The following checklist may assist you in determining the whereabouts of hidden assets or whether they exist.

1. *Financial statements:* Any loans granted to your spouse by lending institutions in prior years required the filling out of sworn financial statements. In most cases, the borrower is trying to impress the lending institution with the extent of assets and may "puff" or overstate the case. In any event, looking back five years or so at these statements may put you on the trail of assets that are at present unaccounted for or that show valuations of assets substantially greater than what is now claimed.

2. *Personal income tax returns:* A review of the personal returns filed by your spouse during the past five years may indicate sources of interest or dividends you didn't know about. You can then trace the disposition of the savings accounts or stocks up to the present time. The returns may also reveal unknown sources of income or loss from trusts, partnerships, or real estate holdings.

3. *Corporate tax returns:* If your spouse is the principal owner of a closely held corporation, he or she may be manipulating salary by taking loans from the corporation or charging personal expenses to corporate accounts that will later be reimbursed or charged to the officer's loan account. Corporate returns should also be checked for excessive or unnecessary retained earnings (undistributed profits), which may disguise available profit distributions or an artificially low salary level. Reimbursement of prior capital contributions or repayment of loans to the corporation may also provide hidden cash flow to your spouse.

4. *Partnership returns:* Examination of your spouse's partnership returns (IRS Forms 1065 and K1) for the years when the returns are available will indicate any sudden changes in his or her partnership interest or distribution. Such changes often occur at the time of a divorce, then compensating adjustments are made after the divorce is completed. Partners are sometimes willing to agree to such arrangements in order to keep you from breaking up or in some manner interfering with the partnership. If business expenses are charged to the partnership, you will want to know the extent of your spouse's charges compared with those of the other partners. The same is true of reimbursed expenses.

5. *Canceled checks and check registers from personal, partnership, and closed corporation accounts:* While time-consuming, it is always reveal-

(continued)

ing to check *all* the canceled checks and bank statements from personal accounts for the past few years, posting the expenditures to different columns on a spreadsheet under utilities, entertainment, loan payments, and so on. You will learn the amount of your total expenditures per year, which sometimes exceeds income, and you will have a better feeling for cost of living and where budget cuts should be made. In terms of hidden assets, you may come across canceled checks for expenditures for the purchase or maintenance of property that you never knew existed. It is important to check the canceled checks off against the appropriate bank statement to make sure that you have *all* of the canceled checks. It is possible that certain checks were removed before they were delivered to you. Bank statements should also be checked for repeated cash deposits or withdrawals. These can indicate that cash is being withheld from deposited checks. It could also mean that your spouse has an outside source of cash that deserves further inquiry. In either case, if cash deposits or withdrawals are substantial and not adequately explained, you can expect a hidden asset or income source somewhere. If your spouse writes checks on a partnership or corporate account where expenditures for the purchase or maintenance of property could be hidden, it is a good idea to check these canceled checks and bank statements as well. You may also uncover expenditures for your spouse's personal benefit that are given false business postings on the corporation books or income tax returns.

6. *Savings account passbooks:* Acquire the passbooks for any savings accounts in which your spouse has had an interest during the past five years or more. Look for any deposits or withdrawals that are unusual in amount, or in pattern. A monthly withdrawal or deposit of money in the same odd amount may reflect mortgage payments or income receipts from sources that you are not aware of. The source or purpose of any such deposits or withdrawals will have to be explained. Substantial cash deposits or withdrawals raise the same questions in both savings and checking accounts.

7. *Securities or commodities account statements:* If your spouse has been buying and selling stocks or bonds or dealing in commodities, the broker with whom he or she trades furnishes monthly or quarterly statements indicating all transactions. A review of these statements going back a few years could reveal the existence of securities of which you had no knowledge or could raise questions about the disposition of stock sale proceeds. Cross-checking securities transactions and bank accounts by date and amount will usually verify the source or disposition of the monies involved. If the securities are sold and the proceeds unaccounted for, you can be sure the money's out there somewhere.

8. *Expense account abuse:* Very often a corporate employer will allow its employees a great deal of leeway in their expense account reporting.

Your spouse may take advantage of this by exaggerating or even falsifying business expenditures. The employer maintains records of expense account disbursements to your spouse over the year with monthly detail. A check of these records will indicate the extent to which your spouse is able to "live off" the expense account and whether there are charges made for dinners in Los Angeles during periods when you know your spouse was home in Cleveland. A cross-check between corporate expense account disbursements and savings or checking account deposits may indicate a pattern of expense account abuse if the deposits exceed legitimate business expenditures.

9. *Deferred salary increase, uncollected bonus, or commissions:* It is always a good idea to check directly by subpoena or otherwise with your spouse's employer to determine whether a salary increase is overdue, when it will be forthcoming, and how much it is. Employers are sometimes sympathetic to their divorcing employees and willing to bend the rules slightly to defer salary increases, bonuses, or commissions in order to suppress apparent income. Ultimately, these increases, bonuses, or commissions must be paid to keep the corporate books straight, and the employer will rarely lie when put under oath or forced to make a written statement on the subject. Sympathy goes just so far.

10. *Safe-deposit box activity:* The bank that maintains your safe-deposit box keeps records of who enters the box and when. These records will not indicate contents of a box or what, if anything, has been removed. If you were aware of the contents at the point when the records indicate your spouse opened the box and something is now missing, you have a pretty good idea of who took it.

11. *Cash transactions and in-kind compensation:* Your spouse may be a physician or a shopkeeper, or in some other work where cash is paid, or he or she may receive in-kind compensation, where something of value other than cash is given in exchange for services. These cash payments or noncash items are rarely reported on income tax returns, but if you know of such income in the past and can subpoena current information, it will help in proving available income in excess of that shown on the income tax returns. If your spouse buys things of substantial value with cash, there is probably a source of cash income somewhere. Most people don't retain cash in a noninterest-bearing form unless they're hiding its source.

12. *Children's bank accounts:* Frequently, a spouse who wishes to hide money will open a custodial account in the name of a child. Deposits and withdrawals are made without any intent that the child have use of the account except in case of the spouse's death. The interest from these accounts is not shown on income tax returns, nor are returns filed for the children. A trace on the source and disposition of these accounts

(continued)

may lead you to other assets. If a parent removes money from what the institution maintains as a "gift-to-minors" account and does not spend it on the child, you can seek a reimbursement on the child's behalf.

13. *Personal knowledge of spouse's habits:* One of the most useful discovery tools is your personal knowledge of your spouse's habits with money. Very seldom will people who are attempting to hide money do so without making some form of written note. When things are going well in a marriage, your spouse may tell you about such records, but you can be sure they will disappear in case of divorce. Look for them in the typical hiding places around the home or office. Make photocopies without your spouse's knowledge, if possible. The more secretive a person is, the more detailed such notes are likely to be. If your spouse has neglected to declare income to Internal Revenue Service, your knowledge of hidden income or assets may prove to be a powerful leverage factor in reaching a satisfactory settlement.

14. *Phony income tax returns:* When the divorce has been filed, some spouses are inclined to alter the *copies* of their previously filed income tax returns in order to hide or adjust pertinent financial information. If you have reason to believe that copies furnished you or your lawyer have been altered, ask for copies of jointly filed returns directly from the Internal Revenue Service. If you are not a signatory to the return, your spouse can be asked to execute the request form. If he or she refuses, you have reason to believe that your suspicions are accurate.

15. *Phony loans or debts:* To keep cash from being divided, a spouse may sometimes attempt to bury it with a phony loan to a cooperative friend or relative. The loan may be tied up with a long-term note or with a claimed likelihood of uncollectibility, so as to remove this money from consideration at settlement time. By having your lawyer question the alleged borrower under oath, you may find that the loan either was never made or was made on the understanding that the money involved would be immediately returned upon request. Using basically the same technique, your spouse may claim a debt to a friend or a relative that must be paid before any division of marital property is made. For example, when a loan is made by a parent or grandparent for the down payment on a house, it is more often than not a gift, with no expectation of repayment. A tip-off to this situation is that only the spouse claiming the debt has signed a note to the relative. The other spouse, who was never aware of the debt or who understood it to be a gift, of course did not sign the note because it probably came into existence *after* the divorce proceedings commenced. Sudden payment of debts to out-of-state creditors who are not available for deposition is usually a sign that the debt is a phony.

16. *"Friends" or other phonies on the payroll:* If your spouse is in a position to control the payroll of a sole proprietorship, partnership, or closely

held corporation, he or she may be paying salaries to a friend or relative who is not actually providing services commensurate with the compensation. The friend on the payroll may be stashing the money away for your spouse or they may both be enjoying it. In either case, the profit of the enterprise will be reduced accordingly and your spouse may be drawing a lesser salary. The same ploy can be used for payment to phony independent contractors.

17. *Retirement plan abuse:* If your spouse has established a pension or profit-sharing plan in connection with a closely held corporation, the plan should be carefully checked to determine whether monies that have been contributed to it are being invested in accordance with the plan requirements. Very often, deductions will be taken for contributions to such plans and then the monies used for personal living expenses or taken out as loans that are never repaid. While the Internal Revenue Service imposes severe penalties if such pension abuse is discovered, these plans do provide an opportunity to secrete assets unless they are closely monitored.

18. *Defined-benefit pension plans:* Defined-benefit pension plans are distinguished from defined-contribution plans by the fact that the benefits payable at retirement age are specified within the plan itself rather than by some contribution formula. The amount of the contributions then must be actuarially determined, based on the age of the intended beneficiary and the point at which benefits are to be paid. A great deal of income can be buried by substantial payments into such a plan in the years preceding or during divorce litigation. The required payments can be a substantial portion of the beneficiary's income, if that is what is required to achieve the defined goal at retirement. This, of course, leaves little money available for support or division as marital property. Once the divorce is completed, the defined-benefit plan can be discarded, even though a substantial tax loss may result. Plans can also be "overfunded" by IRS definition. After the divorce, the spouse will remove the overfunded portion to comply with IRS limits and end up with an asset you were not aware of. Overfunding is a dangerous game because it can result in penalties, including disqualification of the plan for tax deduction purposes.

19. *Gift and inheritance tax returns:* Much useful information is available from inheritance, estate, or gift tax returns of relatives you believe have been generous to your spouse. If these returns show substantial gifts or bequests that have not been accounted for in the settlement negotiations, you are alerted that other assets could also be hidden. A tracing will have to be made from the estate's distribution to see what has happened to the assets.

(continued)

20. *Disgruntled co-workers:* You may be aware of a present or former employee, business partner, or co-worker who is no longer friendly with your spouse. There is a reason for their falling-out, and it usually involves money. If that person feels unfairly treated by your spouse, he or she may provide valuable information regarding hidden assets or income.

CHAPTER IX

You and
Your Lawyer

118. Should I tell my lawyer the whole truth?

Yes. A relationship of trust and credibility is a must between you and your lawyer, and your lawyer has the same obligation to tell you the truth. If you lie about assets or income or other facts, his credibility will be undermined when he deals with your spouse's lawyer, because at some point the facts are likely to come out. If your lawyer suggests that you should lie or tacitly approves misrepresentations, you probably have the wrong lawyer. A competent lawyer does not become enmeshed in the gamesmanship of battling spouses. To the extent that he does, his effectiveness is reduced.

In almost every case your spouse will know when you're lying, even if it can't be proven. The natural reaction to such deception will be countermeasures that are sure to escalate the subterfuge, animosity, and expense. In other words, *you* will be the loser. Make it your rule from the outset to present your lawyer with *all the facts*, then let him worry about protecting your best interests in connection with those facts. He can't anticipate and plan around pitfalls he's not aware of. Also, a lawyer can make reasonably accurate predictions about the outcome of your case only if you give him accurate information to work with.

119. When should I telephone my lawyer?

Your lawyer probably cannot guarantee a time when she will be in the office and available for calls. Many lawyers have to go to court almost every morning, and they have to review files or confer with clients beforehand. Therefore, avoid calls between 9:00 and 10:00 A.M. By the same token, do not call after 5:00 P.M. or at the lawyer's home unless it is an emergency that *must* be dealt with immediately. Most questions have to wait until the next morning to be acted upon anyway.

Ask your lawyer if there is a particular time she will be available for calls—or can return calls. (Some lawyers do return calls in the evening after a hectic day. Others will schedule your return calls if they are frequently out of the office.)

Leave a message with the lawyer's secretary and if possible explain the reason you are calling. The secretary may have the information that you are seeking or be able to get it for you. If so, you can save yourself time and money, because your lawyer working on an hourly fee basis will bill for your call, while her secretary may not. Busy lawyers usually hire secretaries who are really legal assistants capable of dealing with many of your problems.

CAUTION: If your use of the telephone becomes a source of irritation to the lawyer, she will simply avoid that irritation by not returning your calls. Sometimes such an attitude is justified—sometimes it is cause for questioning whether you are receiving the service you need. (See Question 121.)

120. How is my lawyer's secretary important to me?

The secretary is probably aware of your case and of the correspondence and telephone calls between your lawyer and your spouse's lawyer. Although he or she may not be able to discuss the content of these communications, the secretary can reassure you that they took place. Whenever possible, use the secretary (or paralegal if the lawyer has one) for information about calendar dates, court times, depositions, and office appointments. Limit contact with your lawyer to more important matters.

If the secretary finds you easy and reasonable to deal with, your case will get priority. In a well-organized law office the secretary has substantial authority in scheduling appointments, depositions, court dates, and the like. The difficult clients may get poorer service because office personnel avoid them. The lawyer often has time to return only those calls selected by the secretary on a priority basis. Put yourself on the priority list by establishing a positive relationship with the lawyer's secretary.

121. What if my lawyer doesn't return my telephone calls?

The telephone is one of the principal areas of irritation between lawyers and clients in matrimonial cases. The lawyer who regularly fails to return calls and the client who calls daily or at the lawyer's home are equally at fault.

Remember, although this is the only divorce case you have, your lawyer has many more. Do not telephone your attorney to ventilate personal frustration over your broken marriage or the progress of your divorce. Use the phone to exchange necessary information. Handle longer communications by letter or office visit. You have every right to expect your calls to be returned, if not the same day, at least the day after. Begin recording all your telephone calls, indicating the date and the time. If you see a series of logged calls that have not been returned, ask yourself if you have misused the telephone. If so, the lawyer is probably avoiding you. If not, a polite letter outlining the occasions when your calls were not returned will bring your dissatisfaction to your lawyer's attention, and probably earn you special attention.

You will appreciate the lawyer's economical use of the telephone when you're in the office and no outside calls are accepted. Nothing is more irritating than sitting in a lawyer's office and listening to him deal with other cases. If he fills out little pink time slips, every time your appointment is interrupted by a call, remind him to deduct fifteen minutes from *your* bill.

122. Can I call my spouse's lawyer if my lawyer is out of town?

No. And if the lawyer calls your spouse at home and you happen to answer the phone, do not engage in conversation about *any* aspect of the case.

123. What if my lawyer doesn't answer my questions?

Your lawyer may have answered your question but you didn't understand the answer or have forgotten it. These are emotional times, so it is understandable if this occurs. Always prepare and write down specific questions before you meet with or call your lawyer. Once you arrive at the office you may forget many of the questions that were going through your mind at two or three o'clock the previous morning. A lawyer always appreciates the client who prepares a list or agenda for any conference or telephone conversation. There is much less drifting as a result, and you come away feeling satisfied that all questions have been covered.

If an answer to a particular question is not satisfactory or you do not understand the answer, tell your lawyer so immediately. *Don't be afraid to show your lack of understanding.* Your lawyer wants to know when you do not understand aspects of the case. She is paid to know the answers to your questions and to explain them thoroughly, but you must ask the right questions.

CAUTION: People under stress are usually poor listeners. When you ask your lawyer a question, *listen to the answers* rather than thinking ahead to your next question. Don't be afraid to take notes. Again, if you brought a list of questions, you don't have to think ahead to your next one.

124. Does the lawyer ever sell out the client for a bigger fee?

Everyone seems to think so at one point or another. The reason for this is not that there are a lot of dishonest lawyers but that a good matrimonial lawyer does not simply do what the client *wants.* The lawyer is paid by you for special knowledge and professional judgment. Exercising that judgment in your best interests often means *opposing* you. The fact that your lawyer does not share your animosity toward your spouse or your spouse's lawyer doesn't mean he is part of a conspiracy to sell you down the river.

It is not unusual for a litigant to see the issues in black and white. Your lawyer has an obligation to dispel this attitude, to advise you on the strong points of your spouse's case and the weak points of your own. You should appreciate straight advice, because people under stress are prone to self-deception. Lawyers who claim to be representing "the good guy" in every case rarely settle their cases. Their own self-righteousness fuels their clients' emotionalism and misconceptions. They won't compromise because their goals are unrealistic. The result may be an expensive and time-consuming trial before a judge who is likely to be put off by such attitudes.

An effective lawyer will discourage his own client's arbitrary or vindictive demands, and expects the same "client control" from opposing counsel. In that way the potential for amicable settlement or even reconciliation is far greater. This natural difference between a forceful lawyer and an emotional client sometimes leads to unjustified questions about the lawyer's loyalty.

125. What if I don't agree with my lawyer about strategy or tactics?

You should tell your lawyer immediately and give her an opportunity to explain why a particular course should be followed. Although you hired the lawyer for her expertise, you should also explain your opposition to a particular course, because you are the ultimate decision maker. You pay the bills.

A lawyer is justified in refusing to follow a course of action that she feels is unethical or contrary to your best interests. For example, if you feel your children should be called as witnesses to testify on some issue of misconduct by your spouse, and your lawyer resists calling them, discuss this matter with your lawyer. You should be willing to trust your lawyer in matters of strategy and tactics because that is why you hired her. But if you've lost faith in her, or if you can't agree on a point of dispute, consider getting a second legal opinion or hiring a new lawyer.

126. Can I fire my lawyer?

Absolutely. You can hire and fire all the lawyers you can afford to pay. However, if a client has fired more than two or three lawyers, there is probably more wrong with the client than with the lawyers.

If you want to fire your present lawyer, it is advisable to have the next lawyer available to substitute immediately. Hiring multiple lawyers is generally an indication of a controversial contested case, and you should not be left representing yourself for any interim period. Very often, the second lawyer will refuse to become involved in the case until the reasonable fee demands of the first lawyer have been met or arrangements made for payment. In most states the withdrawing lawyer cannot refuse to deliver the contents of your file to the new lawyer, but he may be entitled to go before the court to seek an award of fees and costs advanced on your behalf.

If you don't want to fire your first lawyer but want to bring in a second lawyer for additional expertise, both lawyers can remain in the case and cooperate in your representation. If this procedure is followed, you should have an understanding between the lawyers as to whether or not you will be charged by both of them.

127. Can I get a second legal opinion without firing my lawyer?

Yes. Just go to another lawyer you have reason to believe is competent in the matrimonial field. Tell her the facts as accurately as you can and ask her opinion. Don't be afraid to disclose your present lawyer's advice. The new lawyer should be given all the information she needs to evaluate your presentation of the facts.

While most lawyers don't enjoy second-guessing, the new counsel should be willing to confirm whether the first opinion is reasonable or not. She may even be able to suggest new alternatives, and awareness of alternatives is a prerequisite to good decision making. Your first lawyer may not have explained certain alternatives because she presumed they would be unacceptable to you.

CONSIDER: If you find that you are regularly questioning your lawyer's opinion on matters of professional judgment, she is probably not for you. You should have as much faith in your divorce lawyer as you would in your brain surgeon.

128. Can I object to the fees charged by my lawyer?

Of course, and you *should* complain if the fees are unreasonable. Complain directly to the lawyer if the amount charged is contrary to your understanding with him. If he refuses to or cannot give a reasonable explanation for his fee, you can refuse to pay, forcing him to sue you. The court then determines what the proper fees are and takes into account any valid fee agreement existing between you. Contrary to popular belief, you will have no problem finding a lawyer to represent you over a legitimate fee dispute, and courts lean more toward clients than lawyers in these cases.

Your local bar association probably has a grievance procedure whereby they review fee complaints and sometimes even conduct hearings or arbitrations between lawyer and client. If the lawyer fails to cooperate in those proceedings and the client appears to have a legitimate complaint, the matter is forwarded to the state disciplinary body. They will consider sanctions against the lawyer.

Divorce is such an emotional undertaking that bad feelings or misunderstandings can arise even between clients and their own lawyers, most especially when the question of fees arises. In almost every instance, it is best to work out any disagreement informally with your lawyer. He wants to avoid litigation or bar association inquiries, and you want to avoid paying a lawyer to defend a suit for fees by your previous lawyer—thereby incurring more fees.

129. Is it all right to date or have a sexual relationship with my lawyer?

An ethics opinion in the state of Oregon once held that it is not improper for an attorney to have a sexual relationship with his or her client in a divorce case if children are not involved or as long as the outcome of the case is not affected.

Most people would be appalled at that opinion, and in fact *any* personal relationship between attorney and client is bound to undermine the attorney's objectivity to some degree. The quality of your representation is likely to be adversely affected. Clients are especially vulnerable at this juncture in life, and in most cases it would be unfair for the attorney to take advantage of someone who is emotionally insecure. On the other hand, some emotionally vulnerable clients seem to want their attorneys' personal attentions and encourage special treatment beyond the call of legal representation. In any event, a personal relationship between attorney and client should be discouraged. If the attraction remains after the case is resolved, the parties are free to do as they please.

CHAPTER X

The Case Begins

130. How does a case start?

Usually with the filing of the Complaint for Divorce or Legal Separation. The Complaint and a Summons are then served upon the other party by the sheriff. Without the service of Summons, the court lacks jurisdiction over the other party and cannot order various things to be done, such as the payment of support. If a written appearance is filed voluntarily on behalf of the defendant, personal jurisdiction is achieved and a Summons need not be served.

131. Does it matter who files for the divorce?

In most cases, no. The amount of property and support awards is not affected by whether the plaintiff is the husband or wife. From a leverage standpoint, however, the party who most wants the divorce is likely to give up something during negotiations to get the case over with faster. You may gain some strategic advantage by allowing the other side to file, if you are in no particular hurry.

132. What if my spouse avoids service of Summons?

If your spouse cannot be found by the sheriff within your state for purposes of serving Summons, the court can still grant the divorce. Notice of filing your Complaint must be published in a local newspaper, and a statutory period of time must pass (usually thirty days) to give the other party an opportunity to respond. This is what is commonly called a publication or *default* divorce. The only relief the court can grant by its decree is the divorce itself and custody of children living with you. The court cannot award alimony or child support until the missing spouse is found. If your spouse has property within the state, the court can assume jurisdiction over the property to satisfy support needs.

133. Is it all right to discuss the divorce with my spouse?

Your lawyer would prefer that you not discuss matters involving property or support or matters to be negotiated later. If you are in a fault state, you certainly do not want to discuss grounds with your spouse. The only areas left, therefore, are matters of reconciliation or dealing with the children. The details of the case itself should not be discussed unless your lawyer approves. What you say to your spouse may compromise your negotiating position and may have to be *unsaid* by the lawyer in the negotiating process. When you offer $100 in a casual conversation with your spouse and your attorney intended to offer $70, you may end up paying $125. You just gave the opposition "openers."

Sometimes your lawyer may want to pass along certain information to your spouse through you. Strategically you can affect the negotiations by conveying ideas to your spouse that will get back to the opposing lawyer and influence his perceptions of negotiation priorities. Hints that your job is in jeopardy or that you're being transferred to another state can be conveyed, for example, to make the other side anxious to settle now. When lawyer communications break down, you may want to call your spouse to get things started again. Such strategy should be used *only* under the instruction of your lawyer.

134. Can I discuss my case with friends and relatives?

It would be extraordinary if you didn't. You need to ventilate your fears and frustrations during this difficult period.

CAUTION: The confidant who is a gossip or informant to your spouse can ruin your case. So can you, if you talk too much.

135. What is an uncontested case?

It is any suit for divorce, legal separation, or annulment in which the final judgment is entered *without the necessity of a trial.*

The majority of cases start out to be contested, at least on certain issues. Usually, though, these issues are resolved, and a written agreement is drawn and presented to the court for approval. Thus a contested case has become uncontested (agreed).

The final court hearing required to prove the grounds for divorce and to present the agreement to the judge for approval is not really a trial because everything has already been agreed. When the judge signs the decree of divorce containing the agreement, the case is completed.

136. At what point does my case become contested?

Your case is contested from the moment it is filed until a settlement has been reached. "Contested" simply means that some issues relating to the divorce—custody, property, or support—have not been resolved.

Sometimes there is a contested trial because of a dispute about matters of fact or law that must be submitted to the judge for determination. Other cases go to trial because one or both of the parties are either bluffing or arbitrary in their demands.

137. What is involved in a contested case?

A contested case consists of written pleadings, temporary motions, discovery procedures, settlement negotiations, pretrial hearings, and finally, if all else fails, the trial and judgment of the court. These terms are defined in the Glossary.

REMEMBER: Since every case is contested until the issues are resolved, you proceed as if your case were going to trial until an agreement is reached. The procedures for discovery, negotiation, and temporary motions are essentially the same in all cases. It is the level of cooperation that controls the informality and speed of the proceedings.

138. Is an uncontested case cheaper?

Definitely. Even the simplest case that is agreed at the outset takes from six to ten hours to process, from initial interview to final decree. The variation in charges for such a case is based primarily on the lawyer's time spent advising the clients, suggesting alternatives, and drafting the agreement and decree. If simple forms are used, and most work is done by a paralegal, the cost will be minimal. Most legal clinics handle a divorce case this way. If a case has contested issues and more lawyer's time is required, the cost will increase accordingly.

Even if it is *substantially* agreed, the fees will be higher in a case requiring the skills of the lawyer as a negotiator or tax planner. Although the amount of property transferred and support paid will affect the fees, contingency fee arrangements (where lawyers get a percentage of the settlement) are forbidden for divorce cases in most states.

139. Are there any advantages other than cost in working out a settlement?

Yes. There are several. First, the negotiated settlement will more likely accommodate *your* needs and desires. When your lawyer bargains over particular issues she keeps your priorities in mind, just as the opposing lawyer does for her client. Good negotiators are aware of these priorities and accommodate those that are not in conflict. Those that *are* in conflict must be traded and compromised until the final bargain is reached.

In most cases that come to trial, the judge does not know these priorities because both sides are asking for everything and hoping to get as much as possible. For example, certain items of property will have special intrinsic value to one of the spouses, but the court may have no knowledge of this fact in making its division. The trial judge may believe he or she is giving the wife the better deal by awarding her the main residence and awarding the summer cottage to the husband. But if she has a strong sentimental attachment to the summer home and really has no desire to live in the marital residence, the result is a loss to her. Only through negotiation can the parties accommodate their particular priorities, many of which may have little connection with dollar values.

The second advantage in negotiated settlement is that the lawyers can be more creative in tailoring the settlement agreement to the mutual benefit of the parties. For example, child support and alimony can be paid on an unallocated basis in order that they be fully taxable to the wife and fully deductible to the husband. This can result in a substantial tax savings if the wife has less income than the husband. The tax burden is then shared between the parties at a much lower rate, and the whole family benefits. If the award is left up to the court, there is more likely to be an allocation between alimony and child support, and the Internal Revenue Service will reap the benefits to the detriment of the family. Rarely does a trial judge have the time and sometimes not even the expertise to project the tax results of the settlement he or she orders.

Court-ordered judgments may not be as thorough as carefully drafted settlement agreements, because the lawyers are more or less bound by the findings of the court in drafting the divorce decree. A Settlement Issues Checklist appears on page 109. Trial judges rarely use such a checklist and therefore fail to rule on many of the provisions that could have been added to a negotiated settlement agreement.

Another advantage in negotiating your settlement is the likelihood of greater cooperation in carrying out the terms. Compromise, although painful, more often leads to compliance with the terms because both parties participated in the result. A court decision forced on the parties may leave one or both disgruntled and inclined to resist carrying out the provisions they disliked.

140. What are the pleadings?

They are the papers you file to formally put your case before the court. They tell the judge what relief you want and why.

The initial pleading is usually the Complaint for Divorce (or Petition for Dissolution of Marriage, as it is called in many jurisdictions).

After being served with a Summons and Complaint, your spouse will file a pleading called an Answer (or Response), which either admits or denies the allegations contained in your Complaint.

If new factual matter is raised in the Answer, a Reply may be filed denying that new matter.

These are called the principal pleadings. Once these principal pleadings have been filed and discovery completed, the case is at issue and ready to be tried.

There are other pleadings called Petitions and Motions, which ask for particular relief or raise technical objections to the principal pleading. For instance:

A Motion to Strike or Dismiss a Complaint or Petition may be filed because of some legal defect in the pleading.

A Petition to Show Cause may be filed claiming that one of the parties is in contempt of court for violation of some court order.

Other Petitions are filed seeking particular relief in connection with temporary support, custody, visitation, or injunctions.

Each pleading concludes with a "prayer" or paragraphs that specify the relief requested. Some states require that pleadings containing factual allegations be sworn to or supported by your sworn affidavit. In that case the response to the pleading must also be under oath.

141. What are orders, judgments, and decrees?

They are court rulings put in written form. An order is drafted as a result of a Petition or Motion for some specific relief and submitted to the court for signature. A Decree of Divorce or Judgment for Dissolution is simply a more detailed order, which sets forth the final results of the divorce proceedings, whether by agreement or by contested hearing. Orders, judgments, and decrees must be signed by the judge before they are appealable or enforceable.

142. What is a temporary motion?

It is a proceeding in which a party asks the court for some particular relief before the final judgment for divorce or legal separation. If the hearing requires testimony, the parties and supporting witnesses testify, and the court renders its judgment. A court order is then entered encompassing the details of the judge's ruling.

143. Do you have to give notice to the other side when you file a Motion or Petition?

Once the other side has filed an appearance or been served with Summons, advance notice must be given for any Motion or Petition, except in extreme emergencies or where irreparable injury is likely to result from the notice. *Both* sides must have an opportunity to be heard in court on any issues to be ruled upon by the judge.

144. What is an ex parte motion?

This occurs when no notice is given to the other side because you are seeking emergency relief or because you would suffer irreparable injury if advance notice was given. If, for example, you fear that assets will be hidden, your attorney can petition ex parte for a temporary restraining order forbidding the selling or secreting of those assets. The restraining order is then served on your spouse with a notice of hearing date when he or she will be given an opportunity to object to the order. If the assets are disposed of in the meantime, the court can make the guilty party show cause why he or she should not be held in contempt for willful violation of the order.

A hearing is also ex parte if the other side is given notice but fails to appear.

145. Will I have to testify in connection with my temporary motion or petition?

If a factual issue is involved, someone with knowledge of the relevant facts will have to testify. For example, your testimony will be required to prove your need for temporary support, and your husband or wife will have to testify regarding his or her ability to pay. Failure to present convincing evidence by testimony (or affidavit in some states) will result in a denial of the petition. Failure to offer testimony or other convincing evidence in opposition to the petition will result in the requested relief being granted by default.

146. What information do I need when I apply for temporary alimony or child support?

This is the same information that you were gathering for your lawyer for the initial interview, strictly dollars-and-cents data relating to financial need and ability to pay. Many courts require you to prepare an affidavit detailing your fixed monthly living expenses, as well as all sources of income available to you and your spouse. Even if no affidavit is required, you should bring to court a list of your fixed living expenses (see Income and Expense Affidavit on page 189) and a copy of your latest cumulative paycheck stub. If that is not available, a letter from your employer detailing your gross income and itemized deductions will do. The court will also want a list of liquid assets such as savings and securities, as these may have to be used if income is inadequate. (See the Asset/Liability Worksheet, page 216.)

147. Once a petition for temporary relief is filed, does the judge have to make the decision?

No, the relief requested can still be worked out by agreement of the parties or their lawyers. The petition was probably filed because the parties couldn't agree on a given point. However, once the parties are in court, the pressure of the anticipated hearing with its unpredictable result often produces an agreement before the actual hearing by the judge. In fact many temporary motion judges *require* the lawyers to discuss matters in issue before the hearing and to exchange any relevant discovery information, such as cost of living and the respective incomes of the parties. The temporary motion then becomes a form of discovery and provides a basis for the parties to reach a compromise temporary order.

REMEMBER: It is useful for the parties to learn to compromise now because this stage of the proceeding lays the groundwork for an overall settlement later on.

148. Is there any advantage in reaching agreed orders in connection with temporary motions, as opposed to a decision made by the court?

Lawyers often prefer reaching temporary support arrangements by agreement over letting a judge rule. The judge typically has so many matters pending that he or she does not have time to grant a full hearing on the temporary issue. The judge is more likely to work by rule of thumb, written schedule, or some other timesaving device that might place an unfair burden on one of the parties. When the time gap between a temporary and a final hearing is short, no great harm would be done, but in some jurisdictions years can intervene between a temporary order and the final adjudication.

CAUTION: An inequitable temporary order can place such a burden on one of the parties that he or she is forced into a settlement at a distinct disadvantage. The beneficiary of the order also becomes harder to deal with.

149. What does "without prejudice" mean?

If you enter a temporary order "without prejudice," either party can seek a hearing to modify the order at a future time. Without that language you would have to prove a change in circumstances before the temporary order could be modified or terminated. For example, if you agree to pay $100 temporary child support per week without prejudice, you can later change your mind for *any* reason and obtain a hearing on the amount of support. The "without prejudice" order is binding, however, until terminated or until a new order is entered.

150. Do courts make temporary property divisions?

Almost never. *Use* of property, such as the marital home or an automobile, may be granted by the court on a temporary basis, but the actual award of property is usually reserved until after the judge has decided that there will be a Decree of Divorce.

151. Can the court order my spouse out of the house?

Yes, but most courts are reluctant to do that unless you can prove the likelihood of physical or serious psychological harm from remaining in the same household. A petition for an Order of Protection under the Domestic Violence Act is the usual procedure to remove a spouse from the home when physical abuse occurs or is threatened. The only alternatives are voluntary separation or "self-help." The latter means physically forcing your spouse off the premises or locking him or her out. Self-help is likely to have serious repercussions. Criminal charges can be brought for any physical force used, and changed locks often result in broken windows and doors and sometimes even bones.

When valid reason exists for physical separation, and a court order cannot be immediately obtained, it is probably best for the concerned spouse to leave voluntarily, pending court intervention. But, because leaving the home can have crucial strategic implications in your case, try to check with your lawyer before making the move. *If you are in danger, leave at once.*

152. How are temporary orders enforced?

If either party fails to comply with a provision of an order, a petition for contempt can be filed. The violator then will have to show reasonable cause for not complying or be punished by fine or imprisonment. He or she may also have paychecks and bank accounts garnisheed, and other property may be sold to satisfy unfulfilled financial obligations.

CHAPTER XI

Discovery Procedures

153. How does my lawyer learn the facts about my case?

By following what are called discovery procedures.

Informal discovery begins with the initial interview with your lawyer. Your conversations, then and later, provide information about grounds, assets, expenses, and children. Your lawyer is also learning about *you* in the process—what your priorities are, the nature of your marital problems, and your plans for after divorce. The documentation you provide expands this informal discovery procedure.

If your spouse is cooperating with you in the divorce, his or her lawyer adds to the informal discovery by *voluntarily* providing requested information and documentation.

Formal discovery involves legal procedures such as subpoenas, interrogatories, depositions, and notices to produce documents or things. The current trend is to limit the scope and the time for discovery. Discovery abuse is a major cause of delay and expense in the court system.

154. How does discovery begin?

You have already begun the Asset/Liability discovery process if you used the Hidden Asset Checklist on page 67 and worksheet on page 216 of this book, and brought the information to your lawyer. He may ask you to get more information, which may be available to you without requiring your spouse's cooperation. In the area of grounds, for instance, your friends and relatives may have information about your spouse's conduct when you were not present. Notice may also be served upon your spouse's lawyer, or a subpoena may be served upon individuals or institutions, such as banks, which are not parties to the case, to provide certain information.

Where support or property division are in issue, some states require the parties to file an affidavit of financial condition, detailing their income, assets, and liabilities at the time their initial pleadings are filed or soon after.

155. Do lawyers ever do informal discovery?

Yes. In most cases the lawyers informally exchange information regarding their clients at the outset. The best lawyers do this without hesitation and give complete relevant financial facts. The lawyer knows she will be required to provide this information anyhow, and she can save time for you and herself, as well as the expense of formal discovery. Don't be surprised, then, if your lawyer *insists* that you voluntarily produce income tax returns that you wanted to keep secret, or passbooks to savings accounts your spouse may not know about.

Your lawyer expects to be voluntarily furnished with similar information by opposing counsel with the same degree of candor and completeness.

156. If I ask, will my lawyer help me hide assets or withhold information?

Your lawyer is within his rights not to disclose information that is not requested, but he cannot go along with intentional deception. If your lawyer has a reputation among other lawyers for cooperation in these matters, you will benefit, and information will be exchanged inexpensively.

If you have a lawyer who joins you in concealing information, his reputation probably precedes him, and you can be sure that a substantial amount of *extra* time will be spent in expensive formal discovery procedures. If the opposing counsel *expects* deception, she will spend a lot more time looking for it. Next to trial, haggling over discovery is the most expensive and time-consuming act in most divorce cases.

157. Who is included in the discovery process?

Anybody who knows something that is relevant and important to your case. For example, depending on the issues, one or more of the following might be able to contribute necessary information:

Property division and support: Accountants, appraisers, actuaries, business associates, economists, bank personnel, past and present employers.

Child custody and grounds: Baby-sitters, housekeepers, people who have resided in your home, clergy, neighbors, psychological counselors or therapists, doctors, social service investigators, friends or relatives, your spouse's former friends or lovers, private investigators, police.

158. Are there any benefits from the formal discovery procedures besides information?

Yes. Formal discovery establishes the factual record upon which your agreed settlement is based. In the event of any substantial misrepresentations, this record may be the basis for reconsidering a judgment when a fraud is discovered.

159. Can we settle our case without discovery?

Only if the financial and other facts on which the settlement is based are clear and undisputed. The simpler the case, the less discovery is needed and the more informal it is likely to be. Many cases are settled after a single conference between the parties and their lawyers, but cooperation with voluntary exchange of information is still required.

160. What is a deposition?

It is a statement, taken down in writing, that is your lawyer's primary formal discovery tool. There are two kinds of depositions. In the *evidence deposition*, the testimony is preserved for use at a later court hearing because the witness will not be available. Rules of evidence are strictly adhered to, just as at trial. When the deposition is completed, the testimony is transcribed by the court reporter, sealed in an envelope, and held by the court clerk to be read at the trial.

The *discovery deposition* is used primarily to discover information about issues that may arise in any later court proceeding. A discovery deposition also has a second important function: if you say one thing in the discovery deposition and another thing at the trial, you will have to explain why your answer changed. The parts of the discovery deposition that are in conflict can be read to the witness at trial, and if the change is substantial and unexplained, the overall testimony of the witness is less believable.

161. What types of questions will they ask me at a discovery deposition?

If in your state marital misconduct is important in granting the divorce or awarding custody, property, or support, the lawyer will ask questions that relate to any alleged misbehavior. You will also be asked about income, assets, and financial need, as well as about the care and condition of the children if custody is an issue. A list of sample deposition questions is on page 94.

162. What do I have to bring with me to the deposition?

Only those books, records, and other documents requested by the other lawyer in her Notice of Deposition and approved by your lawyer. Where finances are at issue, you will typically be asked to bring such things as your bank records dating back two or three years, savings account passbooks, deeds, wills, trust agreements, insurance policies, real estate closing statements, financial statements, and the like. If the notice requests documents that are not relevant or that go beyond the bounds of reasonable discovery, the court can be petitioned for an order limiting discovery.

In most jurisdictions it is necessary to bring only those documents that are within your possession or accessible to you. You are not required to prepare documents that do not exist, such as a list of debts or a list of securities owned by you, but it is often a good idea to have such lists anyway. They will help you in the trial of your case and speed up the presentation of that information at the deposition. You can see that in getting ready for the discovery deposition you are actually beginning your preparation for a trial—just in case there is one.

CAUTION: If you fail to produce requested documents or refuse to answer questions, the deposition may be recessed and resumed when information is available. Your failure to present *requested* documentation at the time of deposition may bar you from presenting that same documentation at the trial.

163. May I refuse to allow my spouse to be present when I give my deposition?

No, but other persons who are not parties to the deposition may be excluded. The parties themselves are entitled to be present at all court proceedings and depositions.

164. May I refuse to answer a question at a deposition?

Not unless your lawyer objects to the question and instructs you not to answer it. Remember that the purpose of the deposition is to provide information that will enable the other side to present its case or defend against yours. The questioner is given broad leeway in terms of relevancy to assure that his discovery will be complete. If, on the other hand, the same questions are being asked over and over, or the questioner is harassing you or has gone far beyond what is relevant, your lawyer may interpose an objection to the question. The objection may also be to the form of the question, if it is confusing or improper for some other reason. Your lawyer may instruct you to answer the question over his objection, preserving that objection for the trial, where the judge can then rule whether or not you should have had to answer it. If the judge rules that you should not, that answer cannot be used in the trial to discredit you.

If your lawyer instructs you not to answer a question at the deposition, don't answer it. The questioner may continue with other questions, or she may recess the deposition and file a petition to require that you answer the questions objected to. If the court rules that your refusal was arbitrary or unfounded, fees and court costs may be assessed against you.

CAUTION: If you are apprehensive about certain questions that may be asked at the deposition, discuss them with your lawyer beforehand. He can help you give truthful answers that do the least damage to your case.

DEPOSITION QUESTIONS—SAMPLE

Grounds:

Where the subject matter of the deposition is grounds for divorce, these are some typical questions that may be asked:

PHYSICAL CRUELTY:

Did you strike your wife on or about April 10, 1997?
Did you have an argument with her at that time?
Who was present when you had the argument?
Did anyone witness the striking?
What part of your body came in contact with your wife's on this occasion?
What happened immediately following this incident?
Have there been other occasions when you and your wife have had physical altercations?
When?
Who was present?
What preceded the altercation?
Describe the altercation or striking.
What happened immediately following?

MENTAL CRUELTY:

What are examples of your husband's conduct toward you that you have characterized in your complaint as mental cruelty?
Did anyone witness this conduct? What are the names and addresses of people who have knowledge of this conduct?

ADULTERY:

I show you copies of telephone calls, as furnished by the telephone company, for the months of January through June 1997 and ask you if you are the person who placed the calls to number 835-4059?
Whom did you call at that number?
For what purpose?
Were you driving a 1997 gray Chevrolet automobile with license plate number GN 4037 during the latter half of 1997?
Did you on any occasion park that automobile overnight in the driveway of a residence with the street address 215 South Green Street?
Did you ever spend the night at that residence?
Who else was present?
For what purpose was your automobile parked there?

Property and support

If the deposition is about alimony, child support, or property division, these are some typical questions:

INCOME:

How long have you worked at your present place of employment?

What deductions are taken from your paycheck?

Have you ever received a bonus at this place of employment?

How many exemptions are you currently claiming for withholding purposes?

Have you in any manner altered your working hours since these divorce proceedings were commenced?

For what reason are you earning substantially less currently than you have earned over the preceding three years?

PROPERTY DIVISION:

Is anyone holding any money or property for you?

What was the source of the monies used for the down payment in purchasing your marital residence?

What contribution did your wife make in the operation of your business?

What are your outstanding personal debts and manner of repayment?

Have you incurred any debts since the commencement of these proceedings?

Do you have any debts involving personal friends or relatives?

Are those debts evidenced by promissory notes?

When were those notes drafted and signed?

When was the last time that you borrowed money from a banking institution?

Was a financial statement furnished by you in connection with that loan?

What have you done with the monies that you removed from the joint account you formerly maintained with the children?

What is your estimate of the current market value of the marital home?

Have you had the home appraised within the past twelve months?

What has been the trend of your business in terms of growth over the past five years?

What are your expectations for the coming years and on what factors do you principally base your predictions?

DISSIPATION:

Did your secretary accompany you on your trip to Acapulco in 1995?

Who paid her expenses on the trip?

(continued)

How much did you spend on her for that trip?

Have you ever purchased any gifts for your secretary?

Since your separation, have you taken other people, not including family members, on trips or spent any money for gifts or entertainment for them?

Since the separation, have you loaned money or made cash gifts to your sister?

Have you lost any money gambling since the separation?

Alimony and child support

What are your personal fixed monthly living expenses?

What were you spending annually to maintain the family before the divorce suit? I show you Exhibit A, which purports to be an affidavit by your wife as to her fixed monthly living expenses with the children. Look at that affidavit and tell me of any items contained there that you feel are inaccurate.

Custody

If the discovery issue relates to custody of the children, the following are some questions that might be asked:

Who prepares the meals for the children?

Are they served breakfast every morning?

What is a typical day for you as the mother of the children, starting with your getting up in the morning?

Doesn't the father frequently prepare meals for the children?

What is the quality of his cooking compared with yours?

Doesn't he frequently bathe the children and put them to bed because you are out of the home?

Did you have any conversation with your next-door neighbor within the preceding sixty days regarding your intentions to leave the state with the children?

With whom did you travel when you took the children to Florida for spring vacation this year?

Have the children given you any indication of the parent with whom they prefer to live following the divorce?

Do any of the children have any physical or emotional disabilities or special problems?

Who is principally involved in the discipline of the children?

Calling your attention to on or about June of 1995, did you strike your daughter with a leather belt?

Who was present when this occurred?

Who has knowledge of the allegations that you have made regarding your husband's improper treatment of the children?

Is it not true that your husband is the person in your household who is principally involved with the everyday care of the children?

Is it not true that during the past year you have been away from the home
on an average of three to five evenings per week?

What if anything has your wife ever done that you feel is detrimental to the
children's best interests?

Who would you have care for the children while you are at work if you were
awarded their custody?

Are there services your wife provides for the children that you cannot?

Why haven't you provided these services in the past?

165. Should I volunteer documents and information not specifically requested at the discovery deposition?

In almost every case, no. Do not show the other side *all* the evidence
you have at the deposition. Don't be concerned if your own lawyer
does not ask you the questions you want her to ask, or doesn't ask for the
documents that you feel will prove your case. That information will be
held in reserve for use at an appropriate time. If your case must go to
trial, *surprise* is one of the best weapons in your lawyer's trial arsenal.
That is not to say that you should create surprise by withholding information or making false statements, but you can hide your cards until a
specific request is made to see them.

166. Are there benefits from depositions other than the discovery of information and the preservation of testimony?

Definitely. A deposition helps you and your lawyer prepare for a possible trial in a variety of ways:

1. It helps you evaluate your spouse as a witness.
2. It may give you your first experience as a witness.
3. It will give you a feeling for the strengths and weaknesses of both
your spouse's case and your own.
4. The vulnerability and nervousness people commonly feel at the
deposition can make them more amenable to settlement in preference
to trial.
5. After the taking of depositions your lawyer should be able to give
you an *informed* evaluation of your case.
6. The deposition is a natural setting for settlement discussions.

Even when you feel you don't really need more discovery information, a deposition will sometimes start things rolling by bringing the lawyers and the parties together in a four-way conference setting. Since one of the primary rules of negotiating is not to negotiate until you have all the relevant facts at your disposal, the moment the depositions are completed may be the first opportunity for you all to realistically discuss settlement.

167. Will my lawyer tell me how well I handled the deposition?

If he doesn't tell you, ask him. He may have noticed something that will help or hurt in a trial setting but forgotten to mention it. An honest critique can be reassuring and educational.

168. Are psychological evaluations part of the discovery procedure?

Yes, if someone's mental or emotional well-being is at issue. Most state courts have provisions for voluntary or involuntary psychiatric examinations in connection with matrimonial matters. Local law decides who pays for the examination. An independent psychiatric evaluation is extremely important if there is a serious question of mental health in connection with a custody or visitation issue.

169. How should I prepare for a psychiatric evaluation?

There's probably nothing you can really do in preparation, other than be as calm as possible and honest in your responses to questions. Don't try to "psych out" the evaluator. She does this kind of thing every day and routinely will pick up your attempts to fool her or influence her opinion during an interview. Standard psychiatric tests have built-in safeguards against manipulation by the person being tested. If you attempt to manipulate an evaluation, the test results will probably not be favorable.

170. Is it possible to obtain a second psychiatric opinion?

Yes, when a psychiatric evaluation favors one party on a particular issue, such as child custody, counsel for the other parent can obtain a second psychiatric opinion, which may differ substantially. Having experienced this conflict of psychiatric experts time and again, some trial judges give little weight to *any* psychiatric evaluation unless a serious psychiatric condition is involved.

The results of standard psychological tests are sometimes given more weight in the diagnosis of a specific psychiatric condition because they are less subjective. The more confused a judge becomes from conflicting psychiatric opinions, the more likely he will be to ignore them and fall back on his own experience and common sense in making the final judgment.

171. What is a social service report?

Many divorce courts have the use of a social service agency to make home investigations in child custody disputes. Typically, the investigator interviews the parties, neighbors, teachers, and administrative personnel at the children's school and the children themselves to decide which parent offers the better environment. A written report is then sent to either the court or the lawyers. While these reports are designed to assist in making the custodial decisions, in many jurisdictions the judge is not allowed to read them. The investigator must testify in court and be subject to cross-examination to determine the accuracy and validity of the information or opinions presented. Normally, these investigative reports should not contain opinions on who should get custody, but they frequently do.

172. How do I prepare for a social service investigation?

The investigator will probably visit your home. Your personal appearance, standards of housekeeping, and your children's cleanliness and quality of clothing will be noted. If you are given advance notice of the visit, it doesn't hurt to put your best foot forward by showing the home environment at its *realistic best,* but don't go overboard. Don't create a phony environment where the children wear their Sunday best on a Thursday afternoon and your home is so neat it looks as if no one lives there. Try to have your children present at the interview if you relate well to them. Keep them away if you don't or if you can't control them.

DEPOSITION DO'S AND DON'TS

Preparation

DO — discuss the documents requested at the deposition with your attorney well in advance of the deposition.

DON'T — wait until the day of the deposition to complain that the document production request was onerous or unreasonable.

DO — bring the documents to the deposition as agreed with your attorney.

DON'T — bring your documents to the deposition in a jumbled mess if you mind sitting with two or more attorneys, paralegals, and a court reporter at hundreds of dollars per hour while you organize and search.

DO — organize the documents in folders numbered in the same sequence as the document request.

DO — ask your attorney to file an objection to the production of requested documents to the extent appropriate *before* your deposition.

DON'T — attempt to make a "statement" at the deposition by overdressing or calculated sloppiness.

DO — confer with your attorney before the deposition on questions that are likely to be asked, subjects likely to be covered, and appropriate answers to anticipated questions that may be difficult for you or crucial to your case.

DON'T — try to memorize answers to anticipated questions.

DON'T — worry that your deposition testimony has to be convincing. You are being evaluated as a witness, but you're not on trial—yet.

DON'T — show up late. These people bill by the hour and can make you come back later.

DO — ask your attorney about any legal or factual pitfalls in the deposition and how to avoid them.

DON'T — come to the deposition with an attitude that you're going to show up your spouse or the other attorney.

DO — dress comfortably for the deposition—as if you were going to a nice restaurant for lunch with a friend.

Performance

DO	tell the truth.		DON'T	answer questions with your own questions unless you are seeking clarification.
DO	try to be succinct but complete with your answers.			
			DON'T	try to outsmart the other attorney.
DO	listen to the question and think before you answer.			
			DON'T	allow yourself to be antagonized.
DO	ask to confer with your attorney if you feel it's necessary.			
			DON'T	volunteer more information than is asked for.
DO	ask to take breaks when you're tired.		DON'T	guess or give answers you're not sure of.
DO	try to be yourself.			
			DON'T	object to questions. Your lawyer will do that.
DO	ask to have questions repeated or clarified if necessary.			
			DON'T	refer to documents outside the deposition unless you plan to produce them.
DO	listen carefully if your lawyer makes an objection. She may be telling you something.			
			DON'T	argue with opposing counsel, your spouse, or anyone for that matter.

Remember, depositions can be used to impeach your credibility if you testify differently at the trial. Be correct the first time or preface your testimony with a statement that you're not sure.

---

173. Shouldn't every case be uncontested?

Not necessarily. A fair settlement requires reasonable compromise. If one side is being arbitrary or makes unreasonable demands, a fair settlement may not be possible unless the other spouse shows a willingness to contest the matter and have a judge make the decision. It should be clear that you are willing to go to court if you have to. If it appears that you *won't* go to court, no matter what the circumstances, you severely handicap your lawyer in the negotiation and may even *encourage* excessive demands by your spouse. If the other side remains unreasonable, you can proceed to trial as the final alternative.

CHAPTER XII

Thinking Settlement: Negotiation Strategies and Techniques

174. Will our prenuptial agreement control the terms of settlement?

For the most part yes, if the prenuptial agreement, also referred to as an antenuptial agreement, was entered into without fraud or duress and is not unconscionable in its terms. While premarital agreements were historically considered against public policy and difficult to enforce, they are now favored by most state courts. There is even a Uniform Premarital Agreement Act, which has been adopted by twenty-three states. This will aid consistent application when you are married in one state and divorced in another. Generally, premarital agreements address issues of estate distribution upon death and property distribution in the event of divorce. Premarital agreements can also limit the amount of alimony in case of divorce, but if the limitations are too stringent the court can refuse to enforce them. This is particularly true if a needy spouse is caused undue hardship by circumstances that were not foreseeable when the agreement was entered into. Premarital agreements do not limit the rights of children of the marriage.

175. What is unique about the negotiating in a divorce settlement?

People involved in a divorce usually are so emotional that the process alters normal priorities, clouds judgment, and causes them to take positions that frequently do not represent their own best interests.

For most clients divorce is their first contact with a lawyer or the court system. The uncertainty of the future, the possibility of permanent estrangement from the children, new financial obligations and living arrangements—all arouse fear and a sense of insecurity and loss.

For example, guilt is a major emotional factor in most cases where one party is anxious to have the marriage dissolved and the other is not. The "guilty" party usually is willing to give more and to ask for less in an effort to expiate that feeling. When the guilt subsides, the unfair settlement is regretted and the lawyer is usually blamed. "Why did he let me do that?" the client complains. "I was sold out." By the same token, guilt is exploited by the "wronged" spouse, who feels angry, frustrated, or self-righteous. Virtually no settlement is good enough for the angry client who wants revenge. Such an attitude can lead to expensive and protracted legal procedures with little gained.

Another unique quality of matrimonial negotiations is that there are no objective standards of success. The best result is not necessarily getting the most or paying the least. Spouses who haven't been dealt with fairly have a tendency to try to even up, either by not complying or by trying to modify the decree. Since the parties often continue to have some sort of relationship because of children or some continuing obligation under the decree, a burdensome or inequitable settlement will only sustain acrimony.

176. What are matrimonial settlements based on?

They are based on the respective settlement priorities of the parties balanced by legal norms or standards of fairness in your community. Once your lawyer knows all the facts, she formulates an anticipated result as if the case were tried in court—the legal norm. She then negotiates to achieve your priorities without settling for *less* than the legal norm. If *both* parties feel a little disappointed at the result, the settlement is probably a fair one.

Some mediators say that settlements should be based entirely on the priorities or wishes of the spouses without regard to legal standards of fairness. The problem is that without knowledge of what you are entitled to, you cannot intelligently agree to accept less than the legal norm. *Informed* consent is essential where emotions may control the bargaining.

177. What are the ingredients of a successful negotiation?

Any successful negotiation requires three things:

1. Proper timing
2. Adequate preparation
3. A credible position

Proper timing requires that the parties be psychologically ready for the divorce. Otherwise they will resist any serious negotiation. The clients also should be ready to negotiate *realistically*, rather than emotionally or arbitrarily. If you negotiate at the wrong time, not only will you accomplish nothing but you will lose the advantage by showing your cards too soon. Since *you* are more likely to be emotional or arbitrary than your lawyer, let *him* do the negotiating and determine the proper timing for that negotiation.

Adequate preparation requires knowledge of all the relevant facts, the leverage factors, and your priorities.

A *credible position* means that your demands and the reasons for them are not arbitrary, unrealistic, or untruthful. Only when both sides are credible can you have *serious* negotiations, not merely posturing and jockeying for a dominant position.

178. What are legally relevant facts of a case?

The facts that must be proved for you to gain the legal result you seek. The laws of your state regarding division of property, for example, will determine what facts, such as title or financial contribution, are relevant in the division of a marital home or of stocks and bonds. Because laws vary from state to state, what may be relevant to establish your legal right to the home in New York may be quite different in California.

Being unfamiliar with the law, you are more inclined to think of relevance in terms of emotional or psychological issues rather than legal proof requirements. If you are seeking an award of the marital residence, legally relevant facts relate to (1) title; (2) source of financial contribution; and (3) personal improvement to the property. Legally *irrelevant* facts relate to (1) character of the parties; (2) marital misconduct; and (3) innocence of a party.

179. What is psychological relevance?

This broader relevance takes into account emotional needs and the personal *priorities* of the clients. These may have nothing to do with the law but a great deal to do with the final settlement agreement. All settlements involve the use of leverage factors. The other spouse's priorities and emotional needs may constitute important psychological leverage factors.

For instance, a fear of litigation, a wish to remarry, an obsession for owning a particular item of marital property are all psychologically relevant factors because they can be used to pressure or to gain leverage in negotiation concessions.

180. How do legal and psychological leverage factors affect the settlement?

Anything you control that the other side wants, or vice versa, becomes a leverage factor.

In a fault state the most important legal leverage factor is often who wants the divorce more. If grounds cannot be proved, the other party may be able to delay or defeat a divorce unless the person seeking it makes substantial concessions. If your spouse wants it (to allow remarriage, a move to another state) and you can deny it or delay it—that is a psychological leverage factor. If the facts of your case point to a particular legal result—that is a legal leverage factor.

The art of negotiation is the ability to perceive and use these leverage factors to obtain concessions. Since both sides usually have something the other side wants, these factors are traded like chips. The side with more leverage can obtain more concessions. The end result of the trades and compromises is the settlement.

181. Do plans to remarry affect the settlement negotiations?

Yes, but the manner and extent of the effect depend on the unresolved issues in your case. If, for example, your spouse knows you are eager to remarry, *delay* becomes a leverage factor pressuring you to accept a lesser settlement. Your spouse may purposely delay the resolution of your case for that reason.

In most states, you will not be entitled to alimony after remarriage unless your settlement agreement provides to the contrary. If you are awarded property in lieu of alimony without advising the other side of your immediate intention to remarry, the property award can be set aside in some states on grounds of fraud. The theory is that the court never would have awarded you property in lieu of maintenance (or your spouse never would have agreed to give it to you) if they had been aware of your intention to remarry.

182. When are we prepared to negotiate?

When five requirements have been met:

1. Your lawyer must have the *authority* from you to negotiate.
2. Your lawyer should have all the facts, financial and otherwise, that bear upon the negotiations. The discovery process should be essentially completed. He should also know the law as it applies to those facts.
3. Your lawyer should know all the items or issues to be negotiated in your case. The settlement should be complete, with no unresolved items.
4. Your lawyer should know your priorities regarding those bargaining items. What do you *really* want, as opposed to what you may *say* you want? Your lawyer should know your spouse's priorities, too, in order to recognize a bluff and to put pressure in the area of greatest vulnerability. Certain items may be so cherished that you or your spouse value them far above their intrinsic worth. Those priority items form the bottom line, below which you will not go. (This knowledge represents what were referred to as the psychological leverage factors.)
5. Your lawyer must be aware of the significant *leverage factors* that bear upon the negotiations—your leverage factors as well as your spouse's.

Once these five requirements are met, you and your lawyer are prepared to negotiate. Since timing is the key to successful negotiation, a failure to meet any of these requirements will result in premature negotiations—a less successful settlement or no settlement at all.

183. How do we determine what subjects should be included in the settlement agreement?

We have already discussed many of the possible areas to be included in a settlement. If you have children, custody and visitation must be decided. If you have property, it must be distributed. If you have inherited a summer house and are sentimentally attached to it, this is a bargaining subject. Furniture, summer camp, cars, all can be bargaining subjects—areas in dispute. They may not all be apparent at first, but they will emerge as negotiations begin and information is accumulated.

A settlement agreement should be complete—no loose ends or unresolved problems. Every issue to be resolved, every item of property to be exchanged should be considered and provided for. Where do you start? Try the simple issues first and see how much you can agree on without getting bogged down. There is likely to be a lot of posturing early in a negotiation, when the spouses and their attorneys are most defensive and least willing to show their cards. Looking for areas of agreement at this stage demonstrates a positive approach to settlement, which can disarm defensiveness and promote a spirit of compromise.

Create an agenda of issues with the other side before arguing any substantive dispute. You should go into the negotiation with a written checklist of issues you and your attorney have already discussed. During this feeling-out period, you should add any new issues raised by the other side to your checklist. If you bog down over any issue, put it aside and move on. You may approach issues that have been put aside with a different attitude if other issues have been resolved in the meantime. Issues that might have been "deal breakers" early on may be easily compromised later in a negotiation. If both parties are motivated to settle, resolution of smaller issues can create momentum to resolve the ones that have been set aside.

Always maintain a list of issues and detailed notes of each party's position as the negotiation progresses. Your revised issue list and your position notes will ultimately provide the outline for your settlement agreement.

It is easy to overlook items, and for that reason, we have compiled a comprehensive Settlement Issues Checklist on page 109. Check off any that may apply to your case.

There is always a temptation to defer, until *after* the divorce, certain touchy issues you don't want to raise now. Who pays for parochial school, or your move to another state, or the fact that you are three months pregnant and haven't told anyone? Discuss these issues with your lawyer. Some hidden issues, if raised now, could be used as powerful leverage against you. But most of these touchy issues will be more difficult to resolve later, when you don't have as many unresolved issues to trade. The test is, when will your *leverage* be better? Don't forget the cost, either. Litigation after a decree can cost more than your divorce.

184. Is it more important that my lawyer be a good settlor or a good trial lawyer?

The most successful matrimonial lawyers are the best settlors. A negotiated settlement is far more likely to result in a satisfactory fee for the lawyer and a reasonably satisfied client. Protracted litigation has diminishing returns for both you and your lawyer.

The lawyer's ultimate skill is the art of resolving the apparently unresolvable through negotiation and compromise. His or her trial skills will affect the negotiation if the other side is aware that your lawyer *can* and *will* try the case in court if negotiation demands are arbitrary or unrealistic. In other words, the lawyer must have the skill to negotiate the fair result without a trial—but he or she must be willing and able to try the case in order to achieve that fair result. The trial is the six-gun, which your lawyer hopes won't have to be used to keep the peace.

Although a trial specialist can be brought in at the last moment if negotiations fail, the best lawyers are skilled at both negotiation and trial. (You should find out at the initial interview whether your lawyer is able and willing to go to trial if necessary.)

185. Are the tough negotiators the most successful ones in divorce cases?

No single method is the most successful, and the best negotiators can be hard or soft, as a particular case demands. Whether or not the lawyer is a hard or soft negotiator, a puncher or a counterpuncher, a leader or a follower in terms of negotiating techniques, he or she must properly employ the factors of timing, preparation, and credibility to be successful.

SETTLEMENT ISSUES CHECKLIST

Make your own checklist from the following, selecting what might be relevant to your case.

CHILDREN:

1. Custody (single-parent, joint, split)
2. Visitation (general or specific, notice of change)
3. Support Items:
   a. Weekly, monthly, or semimonthly *support* payment; duration, modifiability, suspension during extended visitation
   b. Ordinary and extraordinary *medical*/dental expense liability; prior notice; health insurance
   c. Liability for *education* costs; private school, college, trade or graduate school; authority to select school; access to school records
   d. Maintenance of *life insurance* for children's benefit; amount, duration, trustee or custodian for proceeds; right to borrow against or switch policies; possession of policies and proof of maintenance
   e. Testamentary provisions for children (*wills*)
   f. Liability for lessons, summer camp, religious training, special needs of disabled children, or other *special costs*
   g. Dependency *exemption*—who claims for this year's and future years' income tax?
4. Agreement or restrictions against *removal* of children's residence to another jurisdiction or state
5. *Restraints* on third-party contact (paramours, friends who may be bad influences) or detrimental activities for children (stay out of taverns, no parachuting)
6. *Rights* of relatives such as grandparents or other interested third parties to have contact with the children.
7. *Sharing* of vital information and/or decisions regarding health and education
8. *Telephone contact*—rights or restrictions in connection with frequency and cost of calls by children or parents

SPOUSAL SUPPORT (ALIMONY/MAINTENANCE)

1. Lump-sum or installment payments for fixed or indefinite period
2. *Amount,* duration, allocation
3. *Modifiability* as to amount or duration in the event of disability, death, or retirement of husband or wife; remarriage; cohabitation; employment; material change in financial condition; emancipation of children

(continued)

4. *Security* for unpaid installments in the event of payor's death or disability (life insurance, securities, other)
5. *Tax effect* of payments
6. *Escalator* or deescalator clauses (automatic increase or decrease)
7. Option to *accelerate* payments
8. Option to *convert* periodic payments to a lesser lump sum at a later date in the event of remarriage of recipient
9. *Life insurance* (amount, duration, policy ownership, beneficiary)
10. Liability for *medical and dental expenses* (ordinary and extraordinary); maintenance or conversion of health insurance to individual coverage
11. Right to *work* (effect on alimony or child support)
12. Testamentary provisions (*wills,* inheritances)

PROPERTY DIVISION

1. Use your Comparative Balance Sheet (p. 186) to identify and classify all assets and liabilities with husband's and wife's opinions of value.
2. Disposition of *real estate:*
   a. Residence—sale, title change, or exclusive possession in one spouse (how long, or subject to what conditions); division of proceeds on sale (what credits to be given for mortgage reduction or improvements)
   b. Other real estate—vacation home, rental property, business property, tax-shelter real estate partnerships
   c. Leaseholds—who is liable for payments, entitled to security deposit, entitled to possession?
   d. Maintenance, repair, insurance costs, real estate taxes, etc.; who is responsible?
   e. Tax liability for capital gains in connection with transfer of appreciated property; deferrability of gain in connection with principal residence
   f. Liability for existing and future mortgages, liens, and encumbrances
   g. Method of conveying real estate (warranty or quitclaim deed)
3. Disposition of *bank accounts* and high-interest investments:
   a. Checking and savings accounts
   b. Money-market accounts, certificates of deposit, treasury bills or notes, commercial paper
   c. Who declares interest for income tax purposes?
4. Disposition of *securities* and corporate holdings:
   a. Is there joint, marital, or community ownership?
   b. Are transfers to be made in kind, in exchange for other assets, or as a division of sale proceeds?
   c. Value of transferred and retained shares
   d. Tax liability for long- and short-term gains

5. Disposition of *partnerships*, joint ventures, sole proprietorships, and other business entities:
   a. Is there joint marital or community ownership?
   b. Value of interest transferred, retained, or released
   c. Tax liability for long- or short-term gains
6. Disposition of miscellaneous personal property:
   a. Pensions, profit sharing, annuities, and IRA accounts (present value; current setoff, or deferred payment)
   b. Household furnishings, tools, gardening equipment, personal effects (description of items; time and manner of delivery)
   c. Antiques, art, collections, and jewelry
   d. Club memberships (use and division of equity)
   e. Disposition of property in revocable trusts or held by third parties as security; accounts receivable
   f. Disposition of vehicles and boats—payment of loans on these
   g. Disposition of royalties, copyrights, patents, or causes of action (lawsuits not brought to judgment)

DEBTS

1. *Schedule of creditors* and balances due
2. *Who will assume?* As of when?
3. Liability for *debts omitted* from schedule
4. Disposition of *security* where one spouse is to pay off secured debt
5. Liability for current and past *income taxes,* assessments, and penalties
6. *Indemnification* and hold harmless in connection with debts to be paid by other spouse

MISCELLANEOUS OPTIONAL PROVISIONS

1. Resumption of *maiden* or former name
2. Whether written agreement is to be *incorporated and merged* in the final decree or remain separate (affects confidentiality of terms and modifiability in some states)
3. *Restraining orders* prohibiting certain conduct (such as altering insurance beneficiaries, etc.)
4. *Arbitration* clause—agreement to arbitrate future disputes out of court
5. *Tax returns*—whether or not to be filed jointly for tax year preceding divorce, as well as indemnification from liability
6. *Security* clause—penalty, setoff, abatement, or funding devices to secure mutual compliance with certain provisions of the decree
7. Attorneys' fees and costs—amount, who pays, and when
8. Attorneys' fees in event of noncompliance—who pays, and under what circumstances

(continued)

9. Release and waiver of claims against the other spouse's property, income, and estate, past, present, or future, except as set forth in the decree
10. *Execution* of documents—time and manner to effectuate provisions of decree

SETTLEMENT PRIORITIES WORKSHEET

Make a list like this one before you enter into negotiations:

A. My priorities in terms of the children are:
  1.
  2.
  3.

B. My spouse's priorities are:
  1.
  2.
  3.

C. My priorities in terms of support are:
  1.
  2.
  3.

D. My spouse's priorities are:
  1.
  2.
  3.

E. My priorities in terms of property division are:
  1.
  2.
  3.
  4.
  5.

F. My spouse's priorities are:
  1.
  2.
  3.
  4.
  5.

Discuss it with your attorney before negotiations begin.

CHAPTER XIII

Talking Settlement: Settlement Conferences and Pretrial Hearings

186. What is mediation?

Mediation is a voluntary procedure in which a couple submits their dispute to a specially trained individual (or team) who helps them reach a settlement. Most mediators are lawyers or mental health professionals, but their role is to *guide* rather than to give advice or provide therapy. People should not enter mediation unless they have determined to dissolve their marriage. A mediated agreement is not binding until it has been presented to the court and approved for entry as a judgment.

187. Do we need lawyers if we mediate?

Yes. Even if the mediator is a lawyer, he or she is not permitted to give legal advice. Although it is not legally required, it is recommended that each spouse have independent legal counsel from the outset of the mediation. In most cases, the lawyers will not be present at the mediation sessions but will help in the discovery process and give legal advice as needed. Mediators who discourage the retention of counsel until the mediation is completed cannot avoid giving legal advice. One person advising two parties with conflicting interests is ethically improper and increases the chance that the mediated agreement will fall apart once the lawyers review it.

188. Is mediation faster or less expensive than the normal manner of resolving divorce disputes?

It can be but don't count on it. Mediators often claim their system is quicker and cheaper, but they are comparing a successful mediation with a contested divorce. If the issues to be mediated are complex, the parties must pay for both the attorneys and the mediator. If the issues are simple, a lawyer can help the parties reach an agreement and complete the court proceedings without the expense of a mediator. If the mediation is unsuccessful, you will still have to pay the mediator's fee and start over again with attorneys. Since there is no way to predict the outcome of mediation, it is hard to generalize about its speed or cost.

189. What are the advantages or disadvantages of mediation?

Proponents of mediation claim that their system has one or more of the following advantages over the adversarial system:

1. The process is less adversarial, therefore less stressful to the spouses and their children.

2. The therapeutic model in communication, cooperation, and compromise enhances the parties' ongoing relationship and their ability to resolve future problems. Even where the mediation is unsuccessful, a therapeutic "halo effect" results in a greater willingness to cooperate and compromise.

3. The use of mental health professionals as mediators adds greater sensitivity to client needs and a superior ability to deal with emotional conflicts in the negotiation process.

4. Mediation is better suited for the resolution of child custody and visitation disputes, where the best interests of the child, rather than those of the parents, should be the goal.

5. Mediated settlements are more creative because the spouses' input is not inhibited by traditional legal approaches.

6. The spouses derive greater satisfaction from the results of mediation than from trials or adversarial settlements because they can give more input and have better control of the process.

7. Mediated settlements result in greater compliance and less relitigation because of the spouses' personal investment.

8. Successful mediations are quicker because the emphasis on co-

operation and compromise encourages early resolution of disputed issues. Less time is spent on discovery and negotiation posturing than is common in the adversarial system.

9. Successful mediations are cheaper because less time and formal discovery are involved, and one mediator costs less than two attorneys.

10. Mediation provides an alternative for consumers that may have a competitive market effect on price.

Those who oppose mediation or support it with reservations suggest some of the following problems:

1. A nonattorney cannot mediate property and support disputes without a thorough knowledge of local law and settlement norms.

2. Ethical problems arise where an attorney-mediator gives legal advice to both parties when they have conflicting interests. A co-mediation with a nonattorney may also raise an ethical problem if the attorney is considered to be practicing law with the layperson. The lay mediator will be guilty of unauthorized practice of law if legal advice is given in the course of mediation. Since it is impossible to mediate any but the simplest marital dispute without knowledge of local legal norms, a lawyer must be available to assist the lay mediator, and two lawyers may be required to avoid conflict-of-interest problems. In the truly simple cases, a mediator is an unnecessary expense.

3. Mediators tend to emphasize *settlement* over *fair settlement* in an effort to achieve a successful mediation.

4. A mediator whose success is based on achieving settlement is more likely to give in to overreaching, or to overlook unfairness when one spouse is arbitrary. Adversarial procedures provide a check and balance in this situation.

5. Mediation requires and presumes good faith and honesty on the part of the participants. In fact, the more serious the marital dispute, the more justified the spouses feel in lying, cheating, and stealing to protect what is "rightfully theirs." If the mediator relies on trust rather than on a healthy skepticism, the dishonest or manipulating spouse will have a distinct advantage.

6. Unless attorneys are employed from the outset, mediation discovery is generally inadequate, and the parties' consent is often uninformed.

7. Two lawyers experienced in family law can be expected to come

up with more settlement alternatives and more creative use of the tax laws than a single mediator.

8. A mediator who does not represent either party cannot provide the emotional support and security available from an attorney who protects the client's interest in the dispute.

9. Unsuccessful mediations are more expensive and require an un-scrambling of the egg as the parties proceed to litigate after undergoing mediation.

10. If the case is simple, one attorney can draft a settlement and prove it up in court faster than a mediator, who must refer the couple to an attorney once the mediation is completed.

190. Can all cases be mediated?

No. The likelihood of a successful mediation depends principally upon the honesty of the participants, their willingness to compromise personal priorities to reach a fair settlement, and the skill of the mediator. The emotionalism and antagonism common to divorcing couples as well as their lack of equal knowledge and bargaining strength reduce the number of cases truly appropriate for mediation. A skilled mediator will generally spot the couples who are not good candidates for mediation, and so advise them at the initial meeting. Mediation does appear to be particularly appropriate to resolve custody and visitation disputes, and many court-sponsored programs are springing up around the country to mediate rather than litigate child-oriented issues.

191. What is arbitration?

Arbitration is a procedure for resolving disputes out of court. Testimony and other evidence is presented to an impartial arbitrator rather than a judge. Unlike mediators, who have only the power of suggestion to reach settlements, arbitrators actually rule on the evidence presented to them. If the parties agree in advance to binding arbitration, they must comply with the arbitrated result once it has been approved by the court. Arbitration of marital disputes is increasingly popular because the parties can choose an arbitrator whose knowledge and experience are tailored to their dispute. Arbitration can also be cheaper than a prolonged court contest because the parties and the arbitrator control the timing of their hearing and the subjects to be resolved.

Many divorce settlement agreements contain a clause requiring the parties to submit certain postdecree disputes to mandatory arbitration.

192. What is a settlement conference?

It is any meeting between lawyers or lawyers and clients to resolve disputed issues. The time and place for these conferences are generally planned in advance, after discovery is complete, but they often occur spontaneously as an outgrowth of a deposition or court hearing. The spontaneous conference is often the most successful because it is motivated by a mutual desire to "get this over with." That attitude is a key settlement ingredient because it suggests a willingness to compromise.

193. What is a pretrial hearing?

It is an informal conference with a judge as mediator. There are two kinds of pretrials: One is purely a settlement conference to resolve anything from a single issue to the entire case; the other is a meeting between the lawyers and the judge immediately before trial to narrow disputed issues to be tried. This chapter deals with the settlement before the trial. Chapter XIV deals with the conference to narrow issues.

194. What is the purpose of the judge's presence if the judge cannot order the settlement?

Influence: The judge has influence over the lawyers and the clients because of official position. The pretrial is an opportunity to learn how a judge would rule on a given factual situation without placing yourself in the jeopardy of a final trial ruling. It is a way to test the water without jumping in. Even when the judge's suggestion is the same as your lawyer's prediction, you are likely to be more influenced by the black robe.

Lack of bias: The pretrial judge can also be helpful in forcing a party or a lawyer who has been arbitrary in the settlement negotiations to be more reasonable.

For example, a wife may believe that she is entitled to one-half of her husband's income for alimony because that is what her friend received or what her mother said she deserved. On the other hand, her husband may believe she should get a job because his boss is a woman. Emotionally distraught clients frequently hear only what they want to hear—the outcome most favorable to *them*. The pretrial judge can dispel any misconceptions because he or she regularly decides divorce disputes and can predict the outcome of your case with authority and without bias.

195. When do pretrial hearings occur?

Whenever the lawyers or the judge wants them to occur. You could be in court on a temporary support motion and the judge might ask the lawyers to step into chambers to see if the motion could better be resolved informally with his or her assistance. Often, if the parties have come on a variety of temporary motions, the judge may suggest that the lawyers and parties sit down with him or her to try to resolve the entire case.

Some courts have pretrial judges who do nothing but conduct informal negotiation sessions in an attempt to resolve entire cases. This kind of settlement conference is generally arranged by the lawyers by mutual agreement after their discovery is complete and after their own settlement negotiations have either failed or achieved only partial success.

196. What information is needed for the pretrial hearing?

Facts: Your lawyer should have a sufficient grasp of the facts, both financial and personal, so that he can employ leverage factors to your best advantage. In most cases, negotiations have occurred before the pretrial, so only the areas of dispute need be presented to the pretrial judge.

Memorandum: Some judges require some form of written memorandum outlining pertinent personal and financial data, as well as the issues to be resolved at the pretrial. Whether required or not, a simple written summary of finances and disputed issues is always an effective way to help the judge understand *your* side of the case. While the other lawyer is arguing the merits of her case, you will often find the judge glancing at the written memorandum. Written memoranda should be exchanged between the two sides before the pretrial to verify accuracy. See page 184 for a sample Pretrial Memorandum.

197. How is the pretrial hearing conducted?

In most cases the hearing occurs in the judge's chambers. The lawyers go in first, without their clients, to give the judge a summary of the case up to that point. Usually the judge is concerned with only the financial factors that are in dispute, rather than with the grounds. However, if you are in a fault state, or if misconduct has bearing on the division of property, child custody, or support, the lawyer should make the misconduct leverage factors known to the judge.

The lawyers give the judge any memoranda they have prepared, and then each one summarizes his or her client's position orally. The judge may question the lawyers for more details or may challenge the legal bases for a particular settlement demand. The judge may "lean on" one or both lawyers by disputing the reasonableness of some position they are taking. If the lawyer gives in to the judge's pressure, a balancing compromise may be sought from the other lawyer, and certain alternatives suggested. Whether the lawyers and judge are strangers or have worked together hundreds of times, a great deal of strategy and technique is involved in getting to what the lawyers maintain is their clients' bottom line—the minimum settlement they will accept.

The next step is for the judge to interview the parties together or individually with their lawyers. (Most judges prefer to interview each of the parties with his or her lawyer present.) During the interviews, the judge gauges the personalities of the parties: some respond best to a soft, reasoning approach; others to a hard, authoritative technique. Some need to be smiled at; others, threatened. Security is the key word with some litigants; jeopardy or fear with others. In any event, the judge, by his own statements and reactions to others', begins the process of persuading the parties or attorneys to compromise their stated demands.

To be effective, the judge may orchestrate the meeting so that, for example, he suggests to the husband, privately, that a trial judge might award as much as $1,000 per month alimony; and then, in his conference with the wife, suggests that the trial might bring only $700 per month. His intention, of course, is that the parties agree to something in between. The judge is not being dishonest, in that there is only a *range* for support, and precise predictions are impossible. A reminder of the extremes can be intimidating to the parties, so compromise becomes a more attractive alternative.

It is essential that the pretrial judge be both knowledgeable as to the law and impartial as to the parties. If he lacks either quality, his effectiveness will be undermined. The clients will not be impressed or persuaded to compromise. The lawyers will discourage their clients' acceptance of judicial suggestions that appear out of line with their experience.

198. Why aren't all the pretrial negotiations out in the open, with everyone present before the judge?

At various stages, private negotiations are more effective. The pretrial may involve a series of separate *and* joint consultations in and out of the chambers to confer with counsel or the judge before compromising on various points. You may prefer to confer privately with your lawyer in matters of strategy or confidence and may prefer private interviews with the judge for the same reason. You and your lawyer and the judge will speak with greater candor when your spouse is not present. The greater your feeling of confidence that the judge *understands* your side of the case, the more susceptible you will be to his or her persuasion.

JUDGE: I'm beginning to appreciate what you've gone through, Mrs. Smith. Your husband is a *very* difficult man to deal with. It might be worth it to take a little less of the property than you're entitled to, just to avoid further aggravation.

MRS. SMITH: I'm so glad you understand, Your Honor. Everyone thinks he's so considerate. But they don't have to live with him every day. How much do you think you could get him to give me?

JUDGE: Well, it's hard to say. His offer is ridiculous, and I wouldn't let you accept it. On the other hand, we don't want to drag you through these courts for months just to prove you're right. How about if I can get him to pay $20,000 and not a penny less. Would you be willing to take it?

MRS. SMITH: Oh, thank you, Your Honor. It's less than I expected, but if you think it's fair . . .

The lawyer then (1) suggests they step outside because she thinks the judge is way out of line and wants the client to hold out; (2) covers her previously too-high prediction by reluctantly agreeing "out of respect for the judge and in the interests of harmony," et cetera; or (3) agrees enthusiastically because the judge's recommendation mirrors the lawyer's and the client needs encouragement.

199. Can there be more than one pretrial hearing?

Yes. Often a series of pretrial hearings is necessary because it takes time to soften the positions of people who are adamant. The passage of time can be a great settlor. Tempers cool, circumstances and attitudes change, new relationships develop, and new perspectives are gained. Even though you may feel the initial pretrial hearing was a waste of time because no one substantially altered his or her position, the seeds of a change in attitude may have been planted. This will make compromise easier later on.

The lawyers should use the time between pretrial hearings to reconsider and perhaps restructure their clients' demands to give them a fresh look when they are next before a pretrial judge. Restructuring the agreement for a client whose pride keeps him or her from compromising will allow change without loss of face.

Again, knowledge of the priorities of both parties is essential to structuring subtle changes in negotiation positions. For example, if a desire to remain in the same house until the children finish school is of greater priority to a parent than money from the sale of the home, a demand for full ownership might be restructured to a half or three-quarter share of sale proceeds deferred for the required number of years.

200. What if my lawyer tells me the settlement is unfair but I want to settle anyway?

Ultimately, you make the decision, but a knowledgeable lawyer will properly discourage you from accepting an unfair agreement. Many clients persist anyway from feelings of guilt, anxiety over pending litigation, or a desire to remarry. But clients who enter into a substantially unfair settlement may in the future blame the lawyer. If you insist on such an agreement, your lawyer may require you to put in writing that you accept the settlement contrary to her or his advice. This protects the lawyer from a later claim that you were sold out or somehow misadvised.

CAUTION: If you have a serious dispute with your lawyer about the fairness of a settlement proposal, or suspect that he prefers trials to settlements, seek a second opinion from another lawyer, not a friend or relative.

201. How do I know whether to accept a proposed settlement or keep on negotiating?

While you may know what you want, you're never sure what you can get. That's why your lawyer's advice is crucial at this point. Regardless of which lawyer drafted the settlement proposal, break down its details into separate items and number them consecutively: (1) custody; (2) visitation; (3) support; et cetera.

Next, consider the questions in the following checklist. Ask your lawyer those questions that relate to a particular item on your list or to the agreement as a whole.

202. Can every case be settled before trial?

No. Some cases can *never* be settled, because of either the personalities of the individuals involved or an honest disagreement as to facts or interpretation of the law. This disagreement can be resolved only by trial. Where only certain issues are disputed, it is possible to try those issues and agree on the rest.

QUESTIONS TO ASK YOUR LAWYER WHEN CONSIDERING A SPECIFIC SETTLEMENT PROPOSITION

When discovery has been completed to the point where you are ready to negotiate seriously, write down the details of any settlement proposal and number the items consecutively. Then, regardless of who is making the offer, consider the following questions for your attorney.

1. In what way is this settlement better or worse than what a court is likely to order if we go to trial?
2. What are the advantages or disadvantages of settling now, as opposed to waiting for trial?
3. Which elements of the settlement do you feel are most important to the other side?
4. Which elements of their offer do you feel are negotiable?
5. Are there any particular elements of their offer that you feel are arbitrary or unfair?
6. Is the amount of money from property division and alimony going to be reduced or otherwise affected by income taxes? If so, how much?
7. Is this the complete settlement or are there items that will be added later?
8. In order to resolve the simple issues, are there items in this settlement offer that we can agree to leaving aside with the unresolved items to be determined by the court?
9. How long will it take to finish the case if we don't settle now? If we do settle now?
10. Do you recommend that we make a counteroffer or delay in some way, if the delay works to our advantage?
11. Is there anything I can do (or stop doing) that will improve our settlement possibilities?
12. Do you feel the settlement is fair, or *better* than fair?
13. Will you be upset, as my attorney, if I refuse this offer? Why?
14. If you were in my place, would you accept this offer? If not, why not?

CHAPTER XIV

Preparing for Trial

203. Do trials take place in states that have no-fault divorce laws?

Yes. While the grounds for divorce may not have to be contested, all other issues that cannot be resolved must be presented to the court for trial. Questions of child custody, visitation, property division, support, and alimony all require trial preparation and presentation in accordance with the procedures and rules of evidence in effect in your jurisdiction.

204. What if my lawyer suggests that another lawyer be hired for the trial?

Such a suggestion means your lawyer is tired of your case or feels inadequate to try it. In either event, look for a trial lawyer immediately. Your present lawyer will probably recommend someone. Get several names, if possible, and follow the search procedure recommended in Chapter III.

205. Do I pay two lawyers?

Yes, unless you discharge the first one; but each lawyer is paid only for the time he or she is actively representing you. Many lawyers use associates and paralegals who perform valuable services at lower rates. Expect to be billed for the time of everyone who works on your case.

206. What does a trial consist of?

A typical trial can be broken down into eight segments:

1. Pretrial conference: The lawyers and trial judge meet to determine what issues must be tried and what facts can be agreed on. Any issues concerning the conduct of the trial can be discussed at this conference.

2. Opening statements: The lawyers summarize what they intend to prove to the judge. When the issues are limited, these statements are often waived.

3. Plaintiff's case: The party who originally filed suit presents evidence in support of the complaint.

4. Defendant's case: The responding party presents evidence to deny or counter the plaintiff's case.

5. Rebuttal by plaintiff: Evidence is offered to deny or counter new matter raised in the defendant's case. (This step is often unnecessary.)

6. Surrebuttal by defendant: Evidence is offered to deny or counter new matter raised in the rebuttal. (This step is unnecessary in most cases.)

7. Closing arguments: The lawyers summarize the evidence presented, in the light most favorable to their clients. Their arguments often impress clients more than they do the judge, who has probably made up his mind by this time. For that reason these arguments are often waived.

8. The judge's ruling (not necessarily on the same day the trial is over).

207. Can the conference immediately before trial be used as a settlement conference?

The trial judge *can* use the pretrial conference for a last-ditch effort at settlement. The issues cannot be examined as closely as they were at the pretrial *hearing*, because this judge's suggestions might be interpreted as prejudicial, and thereby disqualify him or her as the trial judge. This is often a good time to settle, because a willingness to compromise may surface for the first time. In the final preparation for trial, both lawyers and clients often realize the weaknesses in their cases. The risk of a loss or a result less than they originally hoped for will encourage them to avoid the time and expense of a trial. The imminence of trial may also smoke out the bluffers who have held out to the last minute in the hope that the other side will make concessions.

If no settlement is reached at the pretrial conference, at least the trial judge has a better perspective of the overall case and will be better able to evaluate the evidence as it is presented.

208. Are closed hearings available in "awkward" cases?

Yes. If the parties agree to an *in camera* hearing, the judge will generally be willing to hear the matter in chambers or some other suitable closed setting. The lawyers simply have to ask for this type of hearing, indicating why they feel it is necessary and that it is by agreement of the parties. In most cases children are interviewed or testify *in camera* outside the hearing of their parents, in order to avoid the anxiety and embarrassment of a public trial. Statutes in many states provide this protection for children without requiring the agreement of the parents.

209. Must I have witnesses?

No, but witnesses help. In a contested trial the burden is on you to prove your case by a preponderance of the evidence. Issues that involve rebuttal of a legal presumption may require proof by *clear and convincing* evidence. This is a higher standard of proof than *preponderance* of the evidence, which simply means "more likely than not." In either case, if a judge believes your testimony and feels you have proven your case by your testimony alone, no corroborating witnesses are necessary.

The *number* of witnesses presented by either side is not nearly as important as their credibility. The danger of *too many* witnesses is that one or more may be so nervous or verbally inadequate that the overall presentation of your case is diminished. Even a well-prepared witness who is outstanding in the confines of the lawyer's office can freeze on the witness stand and appear to be testifying from a poorly memorized script. One credible witness to a given event may be better than one credible and three partially credible.

Prepare a list of potential witnesses and what issues they can testify about. You and your lawyer can work from this list in selecting witnesses.

210. Should my friends or relatives testify on my behalf as character witnesses?

More than likely your character or your spouse's is not an issue, even in fault states, where marital misconduct must be proven before a divorce will be granted. Therefore, while it is always reassuring to have such support, their testimony will be relevant only if it relates to a particular issue before the court.

211. Can witnesses refuse to testify?

No, not if they are subpoenaed, but if they are angry because you forced them into court, their testimony may be harmful to your case. Some witnesses ask to be subpoenaed so they will not appear to be testifying voluntarily on your behalf. They generally ask when they are on good terms with both parties. They don't want to seem to be taking sides but feel obliged to reveal the truth. Some lawyers furnish all witnesses with subpoenas to avoid the accusation of prejudice that arises when a person testifies voluntarily.

212. Can my former lawyer or a psychiatrist who treated me refuse to testify, even if subpoenaed?

Communications between lawyers and their clients, and between psychiatrists and their patients, are privileged by statute in most states and may not be revealed unless the client or patient waives the privilege. Without this protection you might not be completely candid in your conversations with these people, and the quality of their services might suffer as a result.

You may specifically state that you waive the privilege, or you can waive it by taking some action that is inconsistent with the purpose of the privilege. For example, if someone alleges a psychological condition as proof of mental cruelty or as an excuse for certain behavior, the other side has the right to bring in the attending psychiatrist to verify that condition. If you attempt to justify certain actions by saying that your lawyer told you to take them, you have waived the privilege to the extent that the lawyer may be questioned on that particular point.

CAUTION: The law regarding privilege is a very sensitive one and varies from state to state. If a question arises in your case, your lawyer should be consulted and the statutes and case law of your jurisdiction followed. In some states, for instance, statements made to a treating psychologist or marriage counselor are privileged, even though they contain admissions directly contrary to the allegations and evidence presented to the court. Most marriage counselors will resist testifying in matrimonial matters, claiming a privilege that they may not possess. The danger in forcing them to testify is that they will usually testify favorably to the party they counseled.

213. Will my friends who will be witnesses be able to watch the trial?

At the outset of most trials one or both of the lawyers make a motion to exclude witnesses. This motion is routinely granted, and all witnesses for either side, other than the principal parties themselves, must stay out of the courtroom until it is time for them to testify. Witnesses who remain in the courtroom *after* completing their testimony cannot be recalled for rebuttal or surrebuttal testimony, so it is good practice to ask them to leave.

The obvious purpose of excluding witnesses is to avoid changes in their testimony based on what they hear from the other testimony. Anyone who is not a witness can watch a trial unless it is conducted *in camera*.

214. Can my spouse call me as a witness?

Yes. Each party may call the other as a witness. Because it is expected that spouses will be hostile or uncooperative in answering questions, the opposing lawyer is given greater leeway in the form of questions, and usually she proceeds as if she were cross-examining.

215. Why should any witness be called who is hostile to my side of the case?

The hostile witness may be the only person possessing information essential to your case. Although that witness may not give you certain information, it is hoped that he or she will tell the truth when questioned under oath on a particular point. If the hostile witness does lie, you are not responsible for the testimony, and the judge will have to weigh the witness's credibility along with the other evidence presented on that point. A good reason for calling the opposing spouse as *your* witness may be your expectation of false statements that you have evidence to refute. If you can prove those statements false, your spouse's *overall* credibility is undermined. Even truthful statements may be suspect after a lie has been proven.

216. How is the trial judge chosen?

The assignment procedure varies in different courts. In low-population areas, there may be only one judge who hears all cases. Larger court systems will have as many as twenty judges hearing nothing but divorce, separation, and annulment cases. Some judges will hear only temporary or postdecree motions, and some will hear trials on some system of random assignment. You may not know who your trial judge will be until the day you go to trial.

217. Can I change judges?

A Petition for Change of Venue or Substitution of Judges can be filed before trial begins if you believe that the judge to whom you are assigned is prejudiced against you, or if your lawyer knows the judge's bias will work against you. A hearing may be required before that judge to determine the validity of your charge of prejudice. In most jurisdictions you will be allowed at least one change of venue regardless of cause and without proof of prejudice.

CAUTION: Once trial has begun, a change of judge is allowed only under circumstances so extreme that a mistrial is called for.

218. Can my spouse fix the case?

Sometimes one spouse brags about being able to fix the case in order to intimidate the other. Unfortunately, most people are quite willing to believe that fixing a case is possible.

While it is naïve to suggest that *no* judges are subject to influence, in fact you rarely need consider this possibility, unless the judge's prejudice or refusal to follow the law is apparent. In that case, a change of venue or mistrial should be sought immediately.

If you are concerned about your spouse's threat to fix the case, your lawyer can write your spouse's lawyer a letter setting forth that allegation. If a case is already on trial or assigned to a trial judge, your lawyer can bring the spouse's statement to the attention of the judge, with notice to the opposing lawyer. You can expect a denial of the statement and a good deal of embarrassment. Having been put on notice of the threats, the judge is likely to bend over backward to demonstrate fairness and propriety in the handling of your case.

219. Is it proper for a lawyer to "prepare" a witness to testify?

It is negligent *not* to prepare a witness, unless the testimony is so factually limited that no possible confusion is likely.

The time and method of witness preparation vary among lawyers. Generally, shortly before the trial, the witness comes to the lawyer's office and discusses in detail the issues of the case about which he or she has knowledge. Eyewitness accounts of misconduct, conversations with the other spouse that conflict with current statements, or expert testimony that bears upon custodial fitness are typical kinds of testimony that require advance preparation.

When the witness is interviewed, the lawyer prepares some form of outline of what will be testified to. Putting the testimony in sequence, noting pertinent dates when certain events occurred, and perhaps including key words that will remind the witness of the incident during the trial testimony assist both witness and lawyer in synchronizing their presentation.

If the testimony is extensive, or if the witness is extremely nervous, the lawyer may give the witness a copy of the outline or a list of key questions that will be asked so he or she will feel more confident. Although the witness cannot use this copy to refresh his or her memory on the stand, the advance knowledge of what specifically will be asked builds confidence.

It is also proper to show you or your witness *how* to testify. Presuming the testimony is 100 percent true, it may not *sound* true if presented improperly. There are do's and don'ts in the courtroom, as anywhere else, that determine the credibility and overall effect that each witness has on the outcome of your case.

See Courtroom Do's and Don'ts for You and Your Witnesses on

page 140 and ask your lawyer if she has any to add. For a more detailed guide to courtroom performance, read Hints for Being a Better Witness on page 143.

CAUTION: The preparation just described is not illegal or unethical in the least. Nevertheless, time and again, when asked on cross-examination whether they have discussed this case with anyone, witnesses, with the trial questions burning holes in their pockets, will answer no. They presume from the question that there must be something shady about discussing the testimony beforehand.

220. How do I prepare myself for trial?

Consult the following checklist for questions you may want to ask your lawyer, but in fact you may have to do very little. If you participated in the discovery proceedings and kept up to date with the negotiations, you probably know more about the case than anyone else. It is the selectivity, or narrowing down of the information to the relevant issues, that becomes crucial in presenting a good case in court.

221. What is a trial outline?

It is a script for the conduct of the case. If the case is a simple one, the outline can be kept in your head, and no written document is required. But no matter how experienced or capable the lawyer, the witnesses should know in advance what questions will be asked and what answers expected. Therefore, a pretrial interview and outline of testimony is important for each of the witnesses as well as the lawyer. The outline displays the case in perspective and lets the witnesses see where they fit in the total picture.

The more complicated the litigation, the more valuable the trial outline becomes. It is both an organizational tool and a checklist indicating what details have been completed and what remains to be done. By having this outline available to you at various stages of the proceeding, you have a greater sense of security and awareness of the progress of your case. If a trial actually takes place, the outline enables the lawyer and your witnesses to be on the same wavelength when questions are asked.

See the sample Trial Outlines beginning on page 200.

QUESTIONS TO ASK YOUR LAWYER BEFORE TRIAL

1. What are the main points we are trying to prove?
2. What is my spouse trying to prove?
3. When will *I* testify? How long will I be on the witness stand?
4. Should I memorize anything for the trial?
5. If I get nervous and forget something important on the witness stand, how will you help me remember?
6. If the other lawyer rattles me during cross-examination, how will you help me out?
7. What should I say if the other lawyer asks me _____ (mention the question or questions that you have been fearing most).
8. What questions will the other lawyer probably ask me?
9. What should I bring to court?
10. Can I bring my notes to the witness stand? Can I refer to them from time to time? Can the other side look at my notes?
11. Will I be able to communicate with you when I am on the witness stand?
12. When the trial is in progress and I am *not* on the witness stand, where will I sit in relation to you? Can I talk to you then? How should we communicate?
13. During trial recesses, can I talk to you about my testimony?
14. When should my witnesses come to court? Where should they wait? Can they watch the trial *before* they testify? How about *after* they testify?
15. May I bring a friend or relative who is not going to testify, to be with me for moral support?
16. If there is a custody or visitation issue, should I bring the children to court? If so, when? where?
17. How should I dress for court?

222. What are exhibits?

Exhibits are physical evidence, in the form of letters, deeds, canceled checks, savings account passbooks, or other documentation that is offered in support of your case or in opposition to your spouse's case. Exhibits may also help demonstrate or illustrate points you're trying to explain. They might include photographs, floor plans, financial or other summaries.

For example, you may offer a deed with your name on it as an exhibit to prove that you, rather than your spouse, are the owner of a particular parcel of real estate. You may offer a financial statement your spouse signed to obtain a car loan, which will prove that his net worth is $50,000 rather than $25,000, as he now alleges. A chart may illustrate how the operating expenses of a closely held corporation have grown faster than sales over a period of years.

A point can be made more effectively if visual as well as verbal evidence is offered. Artful use of exhibits frequently controls the outcome of the case. Inanimate objects seem less likely to lie, though, of course, facts that are written down or diagrammed are not necessarily true.

You may want to prepare a list of potential exhibits for your lawyer, indicating what facts they are intended to prove or illustrate. The lawyer will decide which are relevant and admissible as evidence.

223. What is a subpoena?

A subpoena is the court's official way of requiring an individual who is not a party to the action to testify in court or at a deposition. Some forms of subpoena require the witness to bring certain records, documents, or other tangible evidence within their control, such as bank records or photographs.

If the witness has been properly served with the subpoena and fails to appear, a contempt proceeding can be instigated. The sheriff then can take the witness into custody and bring him or her before the court.

If there is a legitimate reason for not honoring a subpoena, such as poor health, the lawyer serving the subpoena should be advised. Any dispute about the legitimacy of the excuse is resolved by the judge if a contempt proceeding is commenced.

224. Can diaries or journals be subpoenaed?

In most cases they can. If you prepare certain documentation for your lawyer *specifically* for the trial or presentation of your case, it may be deemed a "work product" and be privileged against discovery, just as a private communication with your lawyer would be. However, if you look at the diary or journal on the witness stand or in the deposition, you have probably waived your privilege, and the document is subject to scrutiny and questioning by the other side. If the diaries or journals were prepared with no relation to the proceedings, they are subject to discovery.

On deposition you may be asked whether you have any diaries or other memoranda that would refresh your recollection on a given point. If you answer yes, that material may be subject to examination unless you prepared it specifically for your attorney.

CAUTION: Check with your lawyer beforehand if you maintain a personal diary or journal that has entries that may harm your case. There is nothing illegal about disposing of such documentation *before* production has been requested. This is not true, however, regarding business records, canceled checks, and financial records. Destruction of the latter will certainly lead to claims of misrepresentation or fraud, which will hamper your case.

225. Can my diaries or journals be used as evidence if they are stolen by my spouse?

Most states hold that even if evidence is procured by an illegal search or seizure in a civil action (as opposed to a *criminal* action), it is subject to discovery and use in trial if it meets the tests of relevance and authenticity for evidence. (See Witness's Guide to the Rules of Evidence, page 195.)

That calendar on the kitchen wall where you have been noting your bowling activities five nights a week can be offered in evidence to counter your later claim that you bowled only one night a week. Before it is accepted as evidence, your spouse must be prepared to prove that the notations were made by you and that the issue of nights away from home is relevant.

226. I have letters and sworn statements from various witnesses who could not appear at the trial; may I offer these in evidence?

Probably not, unless the other side agrees to the admission of those documents. They are hearsay in nature and do not allow the other side an opportunity for cross-examination to test their truthfulness. Neither does the judge have an opportunity to observe the person who has written the letter or prepared the statement in order to make independent observations as to credibility. The hearsay objection and its exceptions are among the most confusing and misunderstood rules of evidence. They are defined in a simplified form in the Witness's Guide to the Rules of Evidence, page 195.

CHAPTER XV

The Trial

227. What are opening statements?

First the plaintiff's lawyer and then the defendant's lawyer make brief opening statements to the judge, describing what they intend to prove. A good opening statement is a simple synopsis of the case and contains no statements that will not be later supported by evidence. The purpose of the statements is to give the judge an overview of the trial so he or she will appreciate the relevance of the evidence to particular issues. If there has been an extensive pretrial conference, the importance of the opening statement is diminished, and it may be waived altogether. The opening statement should not be an argument on the merits of the case to be presented.

228. Do the witnesses testify in any particular order?

That depends on the lawyer's trial outline, which is prepared in final form immediately before the trial. The order of witnesses is a matter of strategy and technique, with weaker, but necessary, witnesses going first and the stronger witnesses following. If there are a number of witnesses for the plaintiff's case, the plaintiff will most likely testify last, so as to fill in any blanks left by prior witnesses. If there is a particular witness whose testimony is especially powerful, that witness may be saved for last, because the lawyer will want the plaintiff's case to be finished on a high point.

229. What is the difference between direct and cross-examination?

When your lawyer questions witnesses called on your behalf, it is called direct examination. At the conclusion of the direct examination, the other lawyer may question the witness further in an attempt to undermine or discredit the testimony. This is called cross-examination. Witnesses are generally cooperative and straightforward on direct examination but may be evasive or at least defensive on cross-examination. They are aware that the examiner is trying to undermine the credibility of their testimony.

Direct examination: In conducting the direct examination the lawyer cannot put words in the witness's mouth—that is the lawyer cannot *lead* the witness. A leading question would be: "On the first day of May 1997, did your husband strike you with a lead pipe about the face and body and then repeatedly kick you when you fell to the floor?" When the witness predictably answers yes, it is really the lawyer testifying and not the witness. The proper direct question would be: "What occurred between you and your husband on May 1, 1997?"

Cross-examination: On the same event, cross-examination has no such restriction. The lawyer could ask, "Is it not a fact that your husband did not strike you at all on May 1, 1997? Wasn't he defending himself while you struck *him* with a lead pipe?" That question is leading but admissible—because there is no other way to get the information on that point from a presumably hostile witness.

Preparation: You can see why it is crucial that you and your witnesses be prepared for direct examination so you can understand the import of your lawyer's *nonleading* questions and give the expected answers. It is equally important that witnesses be given some idea of what to expect on cross-examination so they aren't taken by surprise or flustered.

Binding testimony: Another difference between direct and cross-examination is that you are *bound* by the testimony of your witnesses on direct examination, even if it is harmful to your case. In other words, the judge will believe the unfavorable things said by a witness who is supposed to be on your side. This is not true on cross-examination or when a witness called to testify on your behalf is so evasive and uncooperative on the stand that the judge declares him or her a hostile witness.

Check the Witness's Guide to the Rules of Evidence (page 195) for a more detailed discussion of evidence problems and solutions.

230. How important is cross-examination?

Cross-examination can hurt your case if the credibility of witnesses is undermined or if they make admissions harmful to your side. On the other hand, cross-examination can help you by expanding and reinforcing the direct testimony.

The good cross-examiner does not go over *every* point brought out on direct testimony. Instead, he or she attacks only areas of direct testimony where some weakness exists, or where there is hope to achieve a particular result (a harmful admission or an incriminating silence). A cross-exam that is an aimless fishing expedition will simply reinforce the direct examination by having it repeated and unshaken. The cross-examiner who takes as much time as or more time than the direct examiner is often conducting an ineffective cross-examination. Another rule of thumb on cross-examination: when the answer is in doubt, it is better not to ask the question. Surprise answers from hostile witnesses usually hurt.

231. Can I turn cross-examination to my advantage and make it support my case?

Yes. Cases are sometimes won on the other side's poor cross-examination. You can prepare with your lawyer certain answers that will score points in favor of your case if you are given the right opening. By asking "what" or "why" questions on cross-examination, the lawyer frequently opens the door to new areas of testimony that could not have been covered on direct examination because of restrictive rules of evidence.

For example, on direct examination you are not permitted to tell what was said in a telephone conversation if it was hearsay. In cross-examination, when you are asked what *you* said, you have an opportunity to get the entire conversation in evidence. "Why did you remove the money from the joint savings account?" might be your chance to respond, "Because when my husband's friend called on the telephone, he said [hearsay on direct examination and inadmissible] that my husband had been threatening to remove the money himself in order to purchase a car for his new girlfriend." Presuming that answer to be true, and actually responsive to the question, the cross-examiner will no doubt cringe.

"What" and "why" questions open the door to all kinds of testimony about motives and intentions. They allow the kind of full answers that may bring out information that can be harmful to the questioner. The witness cannot be stopped as long as the answer is essentially responsive to the question. Such is the price the cross-examiner pays for a bad question.

Demeanor: Your attitude or demeanor under cross-examination can also help your case. Witnesses should assume a manner that suggests the cross-examiner is their friend and they want to be helpful (as far from the truth as that may be). Otherwise, a skillful cross-examiner can undermine the credibility of a truthful witness merely by provoking hostility. If you let the cross-examiner get under your skin, you are far more likely to display a darker side of your character and weaken your case. If the other lawyer believes the direct testimony to be essentially accurate, he or she may deliberately try a few upsetting questions (usually personal or in an accusing tone) just to provoke a hostile reaction and thus reveal you as less amiable than you seemed on direct examination. Refuse to take the bait: display instead an attitude of cooperation. The lawyer will probably quickly terminate the cross-examination. If he or she plods on, your answers will only reinforce the direct examination and might gain you the judge's sympathy or respect if the questioner is obnoxious.

Fortunately for you, most lawyers are not the devastating cross-examiners we see portrayed in movies and television. A reasonably poised witness who is telling the truth will find cross-examination less difficult than direct examination, and the resulting testimony will carry greater weight because it is brought out by the other side.

For a more detailed discussion see the Witness's Guide to the Rules of Evidence, page 195.

COURTROOM DO'S AND DON'TS
FOR YOU AND YOUR WITNESSES

Appearance

DO   dress as you would for an important event.

DO   ask your lawyer's opinion on your clothes in advance.

DON'T   dress down to gain sympathy.

DON'T   overdress to be impressive.

DON'T   chew gum.

Courtroom behavior and courtesy

DO   exercise self-control, no matter what is said.

DO   be punctual for scheduled court appearances.

DO   write your lawyer notes, or wait for a recess.

DO   try to act natural.

DON'T   grimace or react to answers of other witnesses or questions of the other lawyer.

DON'T   whisper in your lawyer's ear during examination of other witnesses.

DON'T   engage in arguments with your spouse or opposing counsel within earshot of the judge.

DON'T   be too sweet and proper, or the judge will think you phony.

Witness stand behavior

DO   your homework.

DO   trust your lawyer to help you remember.

DO   listen to the entire question.

DO   ask to have it repeated or rephrased if you don't understand.

DON'T   memorize answers—it shows, and you may forget the exact words.

DON'T   worry about forgetting.

DON'T   start thinking about your answer before you have heard the whole question.

DON'T   shout. DON'T mumble.

DO	speak up—loudly enough to be heard.		DON'T	look around the court-room while you answer, or at the court reporter, or at your spouse, or at other witnesses.
DO	keep your hands away from your mouth.			
DO	keep your voice modulated, even in the face of intimidation.		DON'T	tell even small lies. If dis-covered, they will taint your credibility on the more significant issues.
DO	look the questioner squarely in the eye.		DON'T	feel the need to explain every answer: "What I mean by that is . . ." sounds evasive.
DO	direct your answers to whoever is asking the questions—or to the judge.			
DO	tell the truth, even when it hurts—the judge will admire that. If the truth will destroy your case, then settle before you get to trial.		DON'T	ask to expand every yes or no answer.
			DON'T	argue with the questioner.
DO	answer yes or no when you can.		DON'T	ask questions back: "What would you do if . . ."
DO	ask if you can expand your answer when you cannot answer yes or no.		DON'T	express personal opinions or conclusions unless they are specifically requested by the lawyer or judge.
DO	trust your lawyer to protect you by objecting to argu-mentative questions.		DON'T	be cute.
			DON'T	be a wise guy.
			DON'T	give flippant answers.
DO	express an opinion if you are an expert on a particular question or subject and it's requested.		DON'T	try to ingratiate yourself with opposing counsel or the judge.
DO	act as if the cross-examiner is your friend and you want to be helpful—this will make his or her job more difficult.		DON'T	be hostile or act as if your spouse's lawyer is the enemy.

(continued)

DO	be straightforward.	DON'T	try to outsmart the other lawyer—or yours either.
DO	answer even those questions that appear insulting or stupid, unless your lawyer objects.	DON'T	assume the lawyer has an ulterior motive for every question.
DO	ask permission of the judge to not answer a specific question—and give the valid reason (for example, that the answer will endanger someone or unnecessarily jeopardize someone's reputation).	DON'T	act defensive or suspicious on cross-examination, by your look or tone of voice.
		DON'T	refuse to answer any question unless you have a valid reason.
DO	answer the question if the judge then instructs you to (or you can be found in contempt).	DON'T	use language that is formal or unnatural—it detracts from your credibility.
DO	use language most comfortable and natural to you.		
DO	tell the story accurately if you are complaining of violent, abusive language that your spouse uses in front of you or the children.	DON'T	be, or pretend to be, too shy or modest to quote the exact words your spouse used when being abusive or vulgar.
DO	say yes if asked whether you have discussed the case with a witness, or whether the witness has discussed the case with you or your lawyer.	DON'T	add unnecessary comments—"And I can prove it!" or "And that's the truth!"—which sound as if everything else you said was unprovable or a lie.
DO	answer a simple yes or no to a tricky question: for example, "Would you have this court believe that..."		

CAUTION: Your conduct in the courtroom or chambers may have more effect on the judge than your testimony.

HINTS FOR BEING A BETTER WITNESS

WHEN YOUR LAWYER IS QUESTIONING YOU
(DIRECT EXAMINATION):

1. Appearance: The first impression you will make on the court is by your physical appearance. Don't dress down for court to gain sympathy. Don't overdress to be impressive. Dress as you would for any important event, such as a job interview or a luncheon with a wealthy relative from whom you hope to inherit. Don't be afraid to ask your lawyer's opinion on your intended clothes for court. Look good!

2. Courtesy: Be punctual for scheduled court appearances. Do not chew gum in court. Do not exhibit hostility or rudeness toward your spouse or your spouse's attorney, no matter how you may feel about them. Assume an attitude of attempting to be helpful when answering questions, without appearing overeager. The judge will have an opportunity from time to time to observe your conduct in court, and your courtesy will make an impression. Judges like nice people, but don't overdo it. Acting like a Goody Two-shoes will appear phony.

3. Preparation: If you have done your homework with your attorney before court you will be less nervous, and the court will appreciate your preparation. A prepared witness does not have to *memorize* answers. If you are telling the truth and have the overall outline of your case in mind, your attorney will make sure that any forgotten points are covered. That's your lawyer's job, so don't you worry about it. If you have carefully thought through the events about which you will testify, you should be able to visualize them at trial, and no memorization will be necessary. If there are lists of items that are involved in your testimony, your attorney can prepare exhibits in advance containing these lists, which you can verify on the witness stand. A witness is expected to be nervous and is expected to forget things. Witnesses who have memorized testimony can usually be spotted immediately by the glassy haze in their eyes as they attempt to recite. Unfortunately, any interruption, especially on cross-examination, may upset the whole train of recollection, and the witness may collapse altogether. Memorizing also causes you to worry about forgetting—and worry makes you forget.

4. Listening: When you are asked a question on the witness stand, don't be thinking about your answer until the question is completed. Listen to the question in its entirety. If you do not understand it, ask to have it repeated or rephrased. Lawyers often ask questions that are too wordy or have too many compound clauses, not because they are trying to be tricky, but because they are not sure of what they want to ask. Most lawyers do not write out their questions in advance, so they are think-

(continued)

ing as they go. Unfortunately, the mouth often moves faster than the brain, and you need not struggle with the muddled result. Just say, "Could you repeat the question, please?" or "I don't understand the question." The court will know if it's a bad question, and so will the lawyer. If a lawyer frequently has to repeat or rephrase his questions because they are muddled, he'll become more nervous than you are, and the judge will be irritated with the questioner—not with you.

5. Volume: Speak up, but don't shout. Keep your hands away from your mouth when you speak, and don't mumble. Your lawyer should adjust your volume as you answer the first few questions put to you, either by asking you to keep your voice up or by moving farther away from you in the courtroom, which has a tendency to increase the witness's volume. Some lawyers on cross-examination have a tendency to shout at the witness in order to be dramatic or intimidating. Should this happen to you, do not shout back. Shouting is an irritation to the court and induces sympathy for the witness. The attorney will likely be reprimanded for such conduct. In the meantime, your carefully modulated responses in the face of such intimidation will make a positive impression. Direct the answers to questions to the attorney who is asking them, or to the judge if the judge is asking them. Do not be looking around the courtroom when you answer, or at the court reporter, or at your spouse, or at other witnesses. Looking the questioner squarely in the eye gives an impression of truthfulness, sincerity, and all sorts of good things.

6. Truthfulness: The keystone of effective testimony is truth—even when it hurts. If the truth will destroy your case, then settle. The lying witness makes a very bad impression on the court, and the results of your case can be seriously affected. Even little white lies can convey the impression of overall untruthfulness and taint the more significant issues. If there are any areas where you fear to tell the truth, make sure to go over them with your attorney in advance. Your lawyer can assist you in answering these questions with the least amount of damage but without your having to tell a falsehood. Ironically, the court sees so much lying that a witness who is particularly candid in response to difficult questions may earn admiration and be rewarded in the ultimate outcome of the suit.

7. Responsiveness: Be direct in your answers to questions. Answer yes or no when you can. Beating around the bush makes you sound as if you are lying even when you are telling the truth. If the question cannot be accurately answered yes or no, then say so. The court will give you an opportunity to expand on your answer. If you repeatedly seek the opportunity to expand on your answer, however, and if in the majority of instances it appears that you could have answered the questions yes or no, you will undermine the effectiveness of your testimony by apparent

evasiveness. It is amazing how witnesses can succinctly answer yes or no to questions on direct examination, then slip into a defensive shell on cross-examination and insist on giving extensive answers to simple questions. The overall effect is the appearance of untruthfulness.

8. Language: Use the phrasing that is most comfortable to you when you are on the witness stand. Language that appears too formal or in any way unnatural to you detracts from the credibility of your testimony. This also means that you should "tell it like it is." If you're complaining about the violent, abusive language that your spouse uses toward you or in front of the children, don't pretend you're too shy to quote the exact words that were used. Your testimony will be more memorable and more credible when you quote exactly.

9. Opinions: If you have expertise in a certain area, you may give expert opinions after a proper foundation has been laid. As a layperson you may also give opinions under certain circumstances where you have personal knowledge of the underlying facts. However, you should avoid spicing your testimony with your personal opinions and conclusions unless they are specifically requested by the attorney or the court. Not only do you violate the rules of evidence when you give an opinion without a proper foundation but if you do it frequently, you may give the impression of being officious or arrogant. It is the court's duty to render opinions on the evidence. Your lay opinion will be requested only where necessary to aid the court in understanding the evidence.

10. Argumentativeness: Don't argue with the questioner or ask questions back. For example, if asked, "What did you do after such and such happened?" don't answer, "Well, what would you do?" If asked, "Did the children visit their father last Sunday?" don't answer, "Well, would you let your children visit someone who has been drinking all afternoon?" Just say no. If the lawyer wants to follow up with a "why?" you can then let loose with both barrels. If the attorney's questions have been argumentative in manner, your attorney will protect you with an objection. Questions like "Were you lying then or are you lying now?" or "Why didn't you take proper care of your children?" are argumentative and objectionable.

11. Acting out: You're as much on trial when you are off the witness stand as when you are on. Don't grimace or shake your head or otherwise react to the answers of other witnesses on the stand or to questions by the other attorney. This kind of playacting inevitably makes a bad impression on the court. It is distracting and has an air of false self-righteousness. The court will form its own opinion as to the truthfulness of the witnesses without help from the peanut gallery. Self-control is not always easy, but it will make you look better than constant upstaging of the witness.

(continued)

WHEN YOUR SPOUSE'S LAWYER IS QUESTIONING YOU
(CROSS-EXAMINATION):

12. Review: Read over hints 1 through 11—they all apply on cross-examination.

13. Conduct: Even though you may believe your spouse's attorney is the enemy, pretend that she is not. Don't be hostile; don't be cute; don't be a wise guy; and by all means, don't try to outsmart the other lawyer. The more hostile the witness, the easier the cross-examination, because that hostility can be exploited. Don't try to guess the ulterior motives to questions, because very often there may be none. A flippant or evasive answer will only give a bad impression—exactly what the attorney wants you to do. Very often, on cross-examination there are no particular facts that can be disputed. But the skillful cross-examiner may still gain ground if you can be provoked into appearing temperamental, stubborn, biased, or evasive. If you can just psych yourself into a frame of mind whereby the cross-examiner is your friend and you wish to be helpful, you will make her job extremely difficult.

14. Refusal: Often a question on cross-examination may appear to you to be insulting or stupid. Answer the question anyhow, if you are able. The judge will sense the stupidity of the question and admire your patience. Don't *you* object to questions, even if they are objectionable. That is your attorney's job, and very often he or she may not make objections for a strategic purpose. At this point you must rely on your lawyer and not take matters into your own hands. If a question is asked that you do not wish to answer for a valid reason, such as unnecessary injury to a third party's reputation, ask permission not to answer the question, stating the reason. If the judge still instructs you to answer the question, do so. Refusal can result in a finding of contempt, or at least give the impression that you're hiding the truth.

15. Defensiveness: Most witnesses tend to be defensive on cross-examination because they are suspicious of the motives of the questioner. The witness most often displays a defensive attitude by evasiveness, hostility, or outright lying. The clever cross-examiner will take advantage of these tendencies by phrasing questions that are argumentative or loaded with presumptions. The best remedy, combined with your determination to be "helpful," is to answer the questions simply, directly, and truthfully. For example, many questions will be opened with the phrase "Would you have this court believe that...?" Right off the bat there is the presumption in the question that you are not to be believed, and the tendency is to argue back. Instead, just answer yes or no and see how devastating the effect can be. "Would you have this court believe that you never struck your wife?" "Would you have this court believe that at no time did you remove monies from your joint

savings account and give them to your girlfriend for safekeeping?" "Would you have this court believe that you never abandoned your children in order to be with your lover?" To all these questions, answer a simple yes if that is the case. If the answer is no, then the attorney must ask additional questions to find out what you *would* have the court believe. At this point you let loose with both barrels of your factual shotgun.

Another common ploy is to ask whether a witness has discussed the case with the party for whom he or she is testifying, or the party's attorney. The answer, obviously, should be yes, but the defensive witness will often be evasive or tell an outright lie. There are many forms of questions that tend to encourage your natural tendency to be defensive, but they are, in reality, forms of trick questions recognized by the court, and it is the manner of your answer as much as the substance that will give an overall positive or negative impression. The real danger for the cross-examiner is that if the questions are answered well, the cross-examination enhances the direct examination rather than undermines it. The skilled cross-examiner will terminate examination when he discovers he is failing to undermine your credibility or composure.

16. Overspeak: Another symptom of defensiveness on cross-examination is the tendency to add unnecessary comments to your testimony. When you finish up a question with "And I can prove it," or "And that's the truth," or "And I have witnesses," you are not underscoring your truthfulness. You are merely suggesting that the rest of your testimony was not truthful, or you were not able to prove it, or not supported by witnesses. When Lily Tomlin, the comedienne, does her routine with the little girl on the big chair, her most outlandish statements are followed up with the famous phrase "And that's the truth." The humorous irony, of course, is the fact that the statement is obviously exaggerated or untrue. Avoid these gratuitous phrases, which have a tendency to give an impression opposite to the one you intended.

17. Opening the door: A basic rule for the cross-examining attorney is never to ask a question if she is not fairly certain of the answer. For that reason, questions that begin with "how" or "why" are always fraught with danger. They open the door for the witness to come forth with seemingly endless self-serving testimony to explain how or why something was done or said. A well-prepared witness will look for these openings in order to get evidence in the record that was not admissible on direct examination because of restrictive rules of evidence. For example, where you are unable to get the content of a conversation with a third party in evidence on your direct testimony because of hearsay, a "what was said" question to any part of the conversation on cross-examination may open the door for the entire conversation going into

(continued)

evidence. Attorneys frequently lose their cases on cross-examination by inadvertently opening the door to areas of testimony that were not otherwise admissible. Once the door has been opened, it cannot be shut as long as your answer is responsive to the question. The seemingly innocuous "Why did you leave the house that evening?" may well cause the attorney to cringe at the five-minute response reciting the fears the witness was experiencing at the vicious conduct of the drunken spouse whose girlfriend had called several times that evening and said she was having an affair, et cetera, et cetera, et cetera.

232. What is an affirmative defense?

In addition to showing why the allegations of the other side are untrue, the defendant's case may bring forth new facts or legal defenses. For example, in fault states, proof of provocation ("He *made* me do it.") may be a legal defense to an allegation of marital misconduct.

An affirmative defense is a direct attack on the plaintiff's case, which, by presenting proof of new factual matter, *legally* bars the plaintiff from the relief sought.

233. What is "counterrelief" in the defendant's case?

If the defendant in addition to answering the complaint asks for relief such as custody, child support, alimony, division of personal property or real estate, he or she will then have to present evidence in support of those counterclaims.

234. Should I be concerned if at the trial my lawyer presents our defense differently from the way we prepared it?

Probably not. A good trial lawyer should be sufficiently flexible to adjust the defense to the evidence presented by the plaintiff as well as to the attitudes of the trial judge. Sensing the judge's attitudes as the case develops is part of the art of trying a case.

For example, reactions to particular witnesses or evidence presented can determine what evidence should be emphasized to satisfy *this particular judge.* If the judge appears to be a strict moralist, you may emphasize marital misconduct as an affirmative defense, hoping to gain sympathy on your behalf. Another judge might be offended or bored by this type of evidence, in which case it is better to play it down or omit it from your defense altogether.

CAUTION: The selection of the trial judge may substantially predetermine the outcome of the case because of that judge's known predilections. Even if you are right as far as the law and the facts are concerned, you may lose the case because the judge was more concerned with evidence that appealed to his or her prejudices. Judges have a great deal of discretion in their interpretation of the facts as they apply to the law in a divorce case. This broad discretion makes appeals based on the judge's interpretation of the facts very difficult to win.

235. Does the completion of the defendant's case end the trial?

No. The plaintiff has the opportunity for rebuttal—to present additional evidence to rebut any *new facts* brought to light in the course of the defendant's presentation. To the extent that the defendant's case merely denies or conflicts with the evidence presented by the plaintiff, no rebuttal is necessary.

Surrebuttal is merely the defendant's opportunity at the end of the rebuttal testimony to present evidence in relation to any *new matter* that was raised in the rebuttal. This part of the trial usually goes rather quickly because the judge, in most cases, has already made up his or her mind and has little patience with additional testimony. If you find that the judge is hurrying the lawyers along in their examinations or sustaining virtually all objections, you can be fairly certain that the decision has been made.

236. What does "off the record" mean?

When a shorthand reporter is making a transcript of the trial, the judge and even the lawyers may ask to go "off the record" in order to make a statement that should not properly be considered by the judge in the conduct of the trial. For example, "What time will we be breaking for lunch today, Your Honor?" is clearly a comment that belongs off the record.

A problem sometimes arises when the trial judge or the opposing lawyer makes frequent comments off the record that may affect the conduct of your case and should therefore be *on the record.* A comment by the judge, for example, about a particular witness or particular evidence that was presented should be on the record because it may affect testimony if the comment is made within a witness's hearing. The comment may also reflect some error or bias in the judge's thinking, which will be grounds for appeal. A judge does not like lawyers to insist that comments be made on the record when he or she has already prefaced the statement with "off the record," and lawyers don't want to anger the judge unnecessarily. Nevertheless, if the judge regularly makes prejudicial comments off the record, it may be necessary to insist they be on the record in order to preserve the record for an appeal.

237. What is a mistrial?

A mistrial occurs when an error is committed that is serious enough that it makes a fair trial impossible. If that happens, one or both of the lawyers, or the judge, makes a motion for mistrial. The proceedings are terminated and reassigned to another judge to begin again. Granting or refusing a motion for mistrial is a matter of the judge's discretion. Mistrials are rarely granted in cases that are not tried before a jury.

238. Why are there so many conferences in chambers with the judge and lawyers during the trial?

In most cases the chamber conferences are an informal method of exchanging information between the judge and the lawyers to expedite the trial. Typical topics are order of the witnesses, anticipated length of testimony, evidence problems, or the hour at which the trial will recess or resume. Judges sometimes get bored hearing a particular case, and the in-chamber conference is in fact a break or social gathering between judge and lawyers at which the case is not discussed at all. This is not a bad idea if the judge's concentration would lag otherwise.

Litigants often become anxious about frequent communications with the judge that are conducted out of their hearing, but they have no reason for concern if both lawyers are present. Most trial judges are sensitive to the litigants' apprehension, and to avoid any suggestion of impropriety will not see either lawyer alone during the conduct of a trial.

239. What are closing arguments?

They are the statements by the respective lawyers summarizing the evidence that has been presented during the trial. Because lawyers are "advocates," each attempts to argue or slant the evidence most favorably toward his or her own client. Misstatements of the evidence are not permitted, but the judge has taken notes during the trial and presumably disregards emotional excesses or inaccuracies.

240. Is there any point in making a closing argument if the judge has already made up his mind?

Unlike jurors at jury trials, judges are not very likely to be swayed by lawyers' closing arguments. Judges are trained and experienced in dealing with complex factual situations and should be able to ferret out the relevant testimony as it is presented in order to come to a conclusion by the time the evidence is completed. However, when a trial is complicated, or has continued over an extended period of time, or involves unique questions of law, the lawyer should insist on the right to a closing argument.

A good closing argument will be more factual than dramatic. The lawyer selects the evidence that is most supportive of his or her case, as well as the evidence that is most detrimental to the opponent's case. When questions of law are involved, the lawyer may argue *particular facts* as they relate to the law or lead to a certain legal conclusion.

A written memorandum of law may be filed with the court before or after closing arguments where legal issues are complex or crucial to the outcome of the case. If the memorandum is filed before, the judge may question the attorneys during their closing arguments to clarify certain points. Some judges even request the attorneys to file proposed findings of fact and law before they rule.

In a long trial, certain bits and pieces of evidence may not seem significant at the time they are presented but become increasingly important as the case unfolds. One can never be sure whether the trial judge has remembered such a small piece of evidence or omitted it from her notes. The trial judge is more likely to be persuaded by a factual argument that assists her in *organizing* the evidence to a logical conclusion than by an argument that is emotional. A closing argument that takes on the aspects of a harangue may be more detrimental than helpful to the overall case.

Since the closing argument is a summation of the evidence, the use of graphs, charts, and written financial summaries can be particularly effective. The judge will welcome anything visual that organizes or clarifies detailed evidence when she retires to her chambers to make a decision.

Clients frequently feel cheated if their lawyers do not make a closing argument, because that is one aspect of trial highly emphasized in the entertainment media. For that reason, the closing argument may be more for the clients' benefit than for the judge's.

241. When does the judge rule?

The judge will rule either at the conclusion of the trial or a short time thereafter if he indicates the matter is being taken "under advisement." The latter phrase means that he wishes to review the evidence before making a final decision. If the judge rules immediately at the end of the trial, without reviewing the evidence, it does not necessarily mean that he has not considered all the evidence.

Most trial judges at the conclusion of the hearing try to find something in their ruling for both parties. Most trial judges prefer that both parties go away a little bit happy—as difficult as that may be. The trial judge is likely not to see the evidence in the blacks and whites that the adversaries do, and therefore makes the ruling in shades of gray. Various compromises may be implicit in the ruling without the judge's actually knowing the clients' true priorities.

242. How does the judge's ruling relate to the final decree?

The last step in the trial process is the drafting and entry of the decree or judgment. The lawyer incorporates the judge's ruling into the decree in the same manner in which he or she would have incorporated the parties' oral agreement had a settlement been reached without trial. A copy of the drafted decree is usually given to opposing counsel in advance for approval. After any disputes have been worked out over the form or substance of the provisions, the decree is presented to the court for entry.

If the lawyers cannot agree on certain provisions, each may submit a decree for entry and the judge can decide which version is proper. The lawyers may conduct an oral argument before the judge in support of their versions of the final decree. The judge can also draft his or her own decree in place of what the lawyers have submitted.

243. What if I don't accept the judge's ruling?

If either party strenuously objects to the court's judgment, a motion to vacate the decree, or a petition for rehearing or to present new evidence, may be filed within term time, which in most states is thirty days from the entry of the decree. If the motion is denied, or if the lawyer determines that nothing can be gained by making such a motion, the lawyer may proceed to file an appeal to a higher court.

244. What are the chances of an appeal's success?

More often than not, when the appeal is based on the trial judge's *interpretation* of the evidence, it will fail. Trial judges are given broad discretion in interpreting evidence because they have the advantage of observing the witnesses as they testify, while appellate judges can only read the testimony. However, if the trial court's ruling is contrary to what the evidence obviously proved (manifest weight), then the appellate court will reverse for "an abuse of discretion."

If, on the other hand, the trial judge has committed some legal or procedural error that has substantially affected the outcome of the case, the chances of the appeal's succeeding are far greater.

Because the cost of an appeal may exceed that of trying the case in a lower court, and because the time consumed in the appellate process may be a year or more, the parties in divorce cases are frequently better off accepting even a bad judgment if they can live with it, rather than prolonging the agony through appeal.

245. Does my divorce lawyer handle the appeal if I want one?

Yes, or your lawyer will assist you in finding appellate counsel. In either case, the fees and costs of the appeal will be in addition to what you originally agreed upon for handling the negotiation and trial. Some lawyers never handle appeals, and others specialize in appellate work.

CHAPTER XVI

Wrap-up

246. When is my divorce decree effective?

You are divorced; the support is to be paid; and the property to be transferred when the judge signs (enters) the decree, unless its specific provisions say otherwise. In some states the original decree is *interlocutory*, which means that a prescribed period of time must pass before a final judgment is entered and before the parties may remarry. Your lawyer will advise if your decree is interlocutory.

Note: Decrees are interlocutory only in the states of California (six months), Massachusetts (six months), Nebraska (six months), and Utah (three months).

247. What happens after the decree for divorce has been entered?

Your lawyer will follow it up by completing the various items called for in the decree, whether it is entered by agreement or after contested trial. This involves the transferring of real estate and personal property, the revising of wills, the modification of insurance policies, and other details that are necessary to complete the physical separation of the parties and the transfer of their property.

See the Windup Checklist (page 160) for a summary of the details that may have to be completed before your case is terminated.

248. What Social Security, retirement, or disability benefits is a divorced spouse entitled to?

Until recently a divorced spouse could not get benefits on the former spouse's earnings record unless the spouse had been contributing to his or her support following the divorce or under a court order to do so. *That support requirement has been eliminated.* For example, a woman who had been denied benefits in the past solely because of this requirement should reapply immediately. Currently, the former wife of a man who is getting retirement or disability benefits is entitled to a benefit on *his* record if she is at least sixty-two years old and had been married to him for at least *ten years*.

249. How about Social Security survivors' benefits?

A divorced wife is entitled to survivors' benefits after the death of her former husband if she is at least sixty years old (fifty if disabled) and was married to her former husband at least ten years; or if she is caring for a child who is either under eighteen or disabled and who is getting benefits on the same record. The child must be her natural or legally adopted son or daughter. Generally, a divorced wife must be unmarried at the time she applies for benefits. The rules on remarriage of divorced wives are the same as those for widows, with one exception: the special provision for widows who remarry at age sixty or later does not apply to divorced wives.

250. May I change my name?

Yes. A name change can be part of your divorce decree upon request. You can also do it later, but there may be additional costs and attorneys' fees. Many mothers choose not to revert to a maiden name in order to save their children the complication of explaining a different name. In most states, you can use whatever name you wish as long as the purpose is not to defraud.

251. Is a spouse required to give back stolen papers used in the divorce?

Yes, if it can be clearly established who owns the papers. Documents that have been marked as exhibits and accepted in evidence may have to remain in the possession of the court until the possibility of appeal has ended. After that period (usually thirty days following the final judgment) each spouse is entitled to his or her own papers and personal effects. Unfortunately, when the parties remain bitter toward each other, these personal items tend to disappear mysteriously.

252. How are modifications made in my divorce decree?

If the modification is by agreement with your former spouse, a court order can be filed detailing the change.

If you don't agree, a petition for modification must be filed, detailing whatever change in circumstances makes this modification necessary. Basically, the only modifiable areas of a final divorce judgment relate to the children and certain types of alimony provisions. The court will conduct a hearing on the contested modification after notice to the objecting spouse, and a court order will be entered granting or denying the relief requested.

253. Is there a period during which my divorce agreement cannot be modified?

Child support payments are generally modifiable upon proof of a substantial change in the children's need, or of a substantial change in the payor's financial ability to pay. The latest child support order was based on the needs of the children and respective financial abilities of the parents *at that time.* Some support orders contain ranges of income where support increases are prohibited or automatically provided for. Courts will generally honor such arrangements but *can* alter them where the children's welfare requires it.

Alimony payments that are not limited as to time or amount are generally modifiable on the same basis as child support and end upon death of either party or remarriage of the recipient. Unlike in child support, the parties can agree in their written settlement that alimony installments are fixed as to number and amount, and they can *prohibit* the court from modifying their alimony agreement. Under some settlements alimony installments may even continue at the same or a lesser rate for a specified period after remarriage—these are called "prodder" provisions, which encourage remarriage.

Unallocated (combined) alimony and child support payments are more complicated in terms of modifiability. Some courts do not accept modification limitations in a written settlement agreement insofar as they attempt to limit child support. However, interpretations are constantly changing in the various states and even in courts within a state. Consult your lawyer whenever you are considering an unallocated support settlement and again when you are seeking modification, because the law may have changed. The tax benefits of unallocated support agreements make them worthwhile even if their modifiability is uncertain.

Property divisions, whether imposed by the court or agreed to by the parties, are not modifiable unless the agreement has some provision for modification based on future contingencies. For example, the wife may be given the residence outright, but the husband will receive a portion of the sale proceeds if she remarries within a specified number of years.

254. Is a husband liable for payment of alimony if his wife is living with another man (or vice versa)?

Living together in the same residence for a continuing period of time causes termination of alimony in those states that have adopted some form of the Uniform Marriage and Dissolution of Marriage Act. In other states, cohabitation may be a basis for terminating or modifying alimony only if the person one is living with provides money for the household, thus reducing the former spouse's need. Either way, the relationship must be of a continuing nature. Modification or termination of alimony is not intended as a punishment for misconduct.

255. What if my spouse doesn't comply with the provisions of the decree, or with any court order?

The court retains jurisdiction over the parties and their children to enforce its orders, judgments, and decrees. A variety of enforcement procedures is available, including garnishment of wages or bank accounts, seizure of property, and imprisonment or fines for willful contempt of court. If your former spouse isn't complying, your lawyer should be promptly consulted for the appropriate time and method for solving the problem. If in your community child support is enforced through the Friend of the Court or state's attorney, that person should be consulted (see Question 70).

256. Who pays for enforcement or modification proceedings?

The spouse in willful violation of a court order may be assessed lawyers' fees and court costs, but ultimately who pays will usually be decided on the basis of financial ability.

The same is true of modifications. Don't be surprised if you have to pay fees even if your spouse is the wrongdoer. The lawyer can't be expected to work for free, and if *you* can't collect from your former spouse, your lawyer is sure to have the same problem. If enforcement is available through the Friend of the Court or state's attorney, no fee is normally charged to the party seeking enforcement.

257. Is inherited property attachable?

Yes. It is subject to satisfying indebtedness or arrearages established by court orders or judgments, the same as any other property. Inherited property has special significance only at the time of division of marital or community property and is generally not included as part of the division.

258. When is my lawyer's representation of me completed?

When the necessary documents are exchanged or recorded, your lawyer closes your file, and his or her representation is completed. Should questions of enforcement or modification of the decree arise at a later time, those are generally considered new legal matters, and if you retain the same lawyer, new financial arrangements must be made.

In most states, notice of a postdecree petition to modify or enforce must be served on the *other spouse* rather than the other lawyer if more than thirty days have passed since the final decree or order was entered. Use the Windup Checklist (page 160) to see that all details are being completed *as soon as* your decree is entered. If there are any errors or misunderstandings in connection with the decree, try to get them resolved or at least in court for resolution within the thirty-day period.

That way you will avoid additional fees and potential jurisdictional problems.

259. Does the entry of the final decree terminate my relationship with my ex-spouse?

Not if you have minor children or if the decree requires a continuing financial relationship between you. Both the welfare of your children and your own peace of mind make it imperative that you and your spouse come to some form of truce. You are not expected to be lovers, or even friends, but why continue the acrimony that probably causes extreme distress to both of you? Your psychological divorce will never be complete as long as you are vindictive toward each other. New marriages or relationships will be jeopardized by lingering bitterness, and noncompliance with the decree's provisions will provide the artillery for a continuing legal war.

260. Are my attorneys' fees and costs in connection with a divorce or separation proceeding tax deductible?

Generally, no, because fees and costs incident to a divorce or separation are personal in nature. However, a spouse receiving taxable alimony payments can deduct the portion of legal fees incurred in connection with the alimony. Likewise, legal fees may be deductible if they are allocable to tax advice or the refund of any tax. You should ask your attorney for a letter or other evidence of that portion of your legal fees that may be tax deductible. The attorney must keep careful time records to support any allocation of time to tax deductible services.

WINDUP CHECKLIST (CLOSING YOUR FILE)

When your final decree has been entered, there will be documents to be prepared by the attorneys and executed by the parties. Some of the documents will have to be recorded and others merely delivered to the other attorney or spouse. The following checklist will help you make sure that no detail has been overlooked. The letters after each item indicate the type of windup activity that may be required to complete your file. Check items that apply to your case (✔):
P = Prepare   E = Execute   R = Record   D = Deliver

1. Real estate

New deeds or assignments (P, E, D, R). Existing deeds, title insurance or abstracts, bills of sale, plats of survey, buyer/seller closing statements, appraisals, leases (D); assignment of leases (E, D); homeowners', renters', owner/landlord/tenant insurance policies (D). Assign beneficial interest to spouse retaining property and deliver cost basis information to compute capital gains or losses.

2. Vehicles

Automobiles, boats, airplanes, trailers, motorcycles, or other vehicles (E, D, R). Confirm insurance coverage and assign beneficial interest (title) to spouse retaining property.

3. Securities

Stock certificates and bonds (E, D, R); assignments separate from stock certificate or bond (P, E, D, R); bearer bonds (D). Deliver certificates or confirm their location in a brokerage house.

4. Insurance

a. Policies of life insurance: ( ) conform beneficiary designations as per decree; ( ) furnish proof of policy maintenance; ( ) consider furnishing insurer with copy of decree if insurance borrowing or modification is restricted; ( ) furnish copy of policy.

b. Policies of health insurance: ( ) conform beneficiary designations as per decree; ( ) furnish proof of policy maintenance; ( ) furnish beneficiary ID card; ( ) furnish copy of policy or schedule of coverage; ( ) furnish conversion documents *immediately* if spouse is converting group policy to individual coverage (there may be a thirty-day limit). Prepare and enter qualified medical child support order.

c. Homeowners', tenants', automobile, or business insurance: ( ) conform beneficiary designations to decree and ( ) deliver policies as required.

5. Debts

( ) Apply for charge cards if you have none *before divorce.* ( ) Inventory balances due creditors as of decree date.

a. Household expenses: ( ) compute the amount due from each spouse on debts to be divided pro rata as of a certain date; ( ) change billing on utilities or charge accounts; ( ) close charge accounts to be terminated; ( ) get final billings; ( ) surrender or destroy charge cards as per decree. ( ) Advise creditors who rendered credit jointly of your nonliability for future debts of spouse. ( ) Furnish statements in your possession for accounts to be paid by other spouse; ( ) obtain statements in spouse's possession for accounts to be paid by you.

b. Loans from third parties: ( ) obtain releases from creditors, if possible, where other spouse is assuming the debt; ( ) obtain written indemnification and hold-harmless from spouse for debts assumed by him or her if not contained in the decree; ( ) change billing address if necessary; ( ) deliver payment booklet, promissory note, mortgage, or other documentation to party assuming debt; ( ) consider letter to creditor advising of spouse's assumption of liability and requesting notice in event of default before institution of any collection procedures.

c. Debts between spouses: ( ) P ( ) E ( ) D, any notes to be exchanged between spouses as part of property settlement; ( ) verify that any security devices (to guarantee specified payments) called for under decree have been executed or effectuated as required, e.g., lien on real estate or maintenance of life insurance in amount equal to unpaid balance of lump-sum settlement to be paid in future installments.

6. Bank accounts, CD's, and so on

a. Savings account passbooks: ( ) D, conform account ownership to decree; ( ) verify balance as per decree or agreement; ( ) consider reinvestment for higher yield.

b. Certificates of deposit: ( ) D, conform account ownership with decree.

c. Treasury bills and notes: ( ) D, conform ownership with decree.

d. Checking accounts: ( ) D, canceled checks and bank statements; ( ) conform account title with decree; ( ) close or remove name from accounts that spouse could overdraft.

e. Money-market accounts: ( ) conform account ownership with decree and ( ) D.

(continued)

7. Income tax

( ) Verify whether joint return is to be filed with spouse, disposition of refund or liability; who is to prepare return; ( ) D, supporting income and deduction documentation. ( ) Obtain hold-harmless and indemnification for tax liability in past years if appropriate. ( ) Clarify tax liability for exchanges of property under divorce decree, year of declaration, and possible exemption or deferral of tax. ( ) Clarify tax liability from alimony or periodic payments; ( ) arrange for tax reserve in proper amount and filing of quarterly estimates. ( ) Obtain cost basis information for appreciated or depreciated real estate or investments.

8. Estate planning

( ) Consult with attorney regarding necessity of will; ( ) revise estate plan if appropriate and consider investment advice as to any assets from marital settlement not needed for current living expenses. ( ) Depending on size and complexity of estate, an attorney, accountant, or financial consultant may be advisable to set you on the right financial track from the outset of the divorce.

9. Trusts

Assignments of beneficial interest or powers of direction for existing trusts ( ) P; ( ) E; ( ) D. New trust agreements to secure alimony, child support, educational needs, or some testamentary purpose ( ) P; E; ( ) D.

10. Personal property exchange

Household furnishings, personal effects, tools, jewelry ( ). Arrange time and place for pickup or delivery.

11. Retirement benefits

Prepare and enter Qualified Domestic Relations Order (QDRO), send to plan administrator for approval, and transfer IRA and other retirement benefits as required under the decree.

QUESTIONS TO ASK YOUR LAWYER
UPON ENTRY OF THE FINAL DECREE

When your case has been completed and your final decree entered, you still have to record deeds, deliver documents and property, and pay monies due. The following questions should give you perspective on what to expect in your new divorced status and assist the windup of your file.

1. When is my decree for divorce, separate maintenance, or annulment final or effective? When will I receive a copy of the decree?
2. When can I remarry?
3. When are support payments due? How should I keep track of the payments, and how should they be allocated to alimony or child support? Who claims the dependent tax exemption for the children?
4. What documents should I receive from transfers of real estate, vehicles, securities, insurance policies, and the like? What documents am I to execute? Who will prepare these documents? Who will record them?
5. What is the balance of my attorneys' fees and costs? Are there any additional fees or cost charges in connection with the windup of the case?
6. When should I expect other personal property, such as furniture, to be picked up or delivered? Who is responsible for delivery arrangements and costs?
7. If my spouse is not complying with the decree in the matter of support payments or delivery of property or documents, what should I do?
8. Who will pay the attorneys' fees and court costs in connection with any enforcement proceedings?
9. Now that I am divorced, should I have a will or should my present will be revised?
10. Can I file a joint income-tax return for this year? What records should I keep for income tax in future years?
11. Can I take the children out of town for vacations?
12. Can my girlfriend or boyfriend come along on visitation?
13. How will a live-in girlfriend or boyfriend affect custody rights?
14. When can I start collecting retirement benefits?

Checklists, Schedules, Guides, and Court Documents

RECONCILIATION GUIDE

While it is virtually impossible to force a reconciliation if one party is committed to a divorce, a mutual effort to resolve your marital problems constructively provides the best opportunity for a positive outcome. Here are some practical suggestions:

EASE UP

Give your spouse some breathing room. Constant pressure to reconcile, tears, threats, or begging are more likely to bury your dying marriage than resurrect it. Remember, spouses who are already thinking of divorce feel threatened by the very idea of reconciliation. So talk in terms of constructive resolutions to your problems that may or may not include reconciliation.

STOP BLAMING

No marriage has ever been saved by identifying the "bad guy." Blame is destructive to relationships whether it's directed at your spouse or yourself. Fault has no place in constructive resolutions.

GET HELP

Get the help of a trained and experienced marriage therapist to help you through this hard time. It doesn't matter whether you choose a psychiatrist, a psychologist, or a social worker as long as training, experience, and the ability to communicate are there. Choose a therapist who is willing to see you and your spouse individually and together when that's appropriate. Choose a counselor that both you and your spouse will feel comfortable with.

Deflect resistance from your spouse by emphasis on constructive resolutions rather than reconciliation.

MAKE A DEAL

Make a deal with your spouse. Promise that you won't fight the fact of a divorce if she or he will delay the proceeding long enough to evaluate the possibility of constructive resolutions. Don't expect a commitment to reconcile at this point—only an effort to explore the possibilities. The goal is to get both of you into therapy for an evaluation.

UNDERTAKE A MARITAL EVALUATION

As part of the bargain, your spouse must agree to meet with the marriage therapist for enough sessions to evaluate your potential for constructive resolutions. Ask the therapist to ensure the confidentiality of the individual sessions or your spouse won't be candid and may not participate at all.

HIT THE BOOKS

Take a trip to the library or the local bookstore and do some reading about communication and why marriages fail. See the Bibliography and ask your therapist to suggest some titles.

LEARN TO LISTEN

Poor communication is the gangrene of dying marriages. The biggest problem is not what's *said*. It's what's *not heard*. Learn to talk one at a time and to listen all the time.

TRY TO UNDERSTAND

Try to understand your spouse's feelings and needs as well as your own. If you can't relate to your spouse's feelings, constructive resolutions are not likely and reconciliation may not even be advisable.

SHOW RESPECT

Respect your spouse and her or his feelings. You can respect another point of view without agreeing with it. If you can't show respect, what's the point of reconciling?

TRY TO TRUST

Try to trust your spouse even if you've been disappointed in the past. Respect and trust are the lubricants of marital conflict. They inspire the hope and confidence that make constructive resolutions possible.

FORGIVE AND FORGET

While your marriage was breaking down, you and your spouse may have said or done some "unforgivable" things. Well, you are going to have to forgive *and forget*. If you don't, your spouse will know it and will probably come up with something unforgivable and unforgettable about you. In that case, forget about reconciliation.

DON'T MOPE

Don't mope or grouse around the house while you are in counseling. Depressed, angry, or self-righteous people are not fun to be around and are lousy candidates for reconciliation. Ask your therapist to help you with your depression, your anger, or other emotions that handicap your potential for constructive resolutions. There's more than a marriage at stake here.

GET A LIFE

Develop some independence from your spouse and interests outside your marriage. You'll feel better about yourself and may become more interesting to your spouse in the process.

BE REALISTIC

Recognize that even if reconciliation is impossible for you two, constructive resolutions to your marital problems will improve the quality of life for you and those around you. If you're not progressing toward a better marriage, see if your therapist can prepare you and your spouse for a better divorce. That's a constructive resolution when reconciliation isn't in the cards.

INFORMATION FREQUENTLY REQUESTED AT YOUR INITIAL INTERVIEW

PERSONAL BACKGROUND

1. Names and addresses of spouses
2. Maiden name of wife
3. Dates and places of birth of spouses
4. Religions of spouses
5. Residence phones of spouses
6. Business phones of spouses
7. Personal health of spouses, with details of any extraordinary physical or psychological problems
8. Educational background of spouses and special training, if any
9. Date and place of marriage to current spouse and number of prior marriages and how terminated
10. Address to which mail should be directed, if not the residence address, and telephone numbers where client may be contacted, if not the residence or work phone number
11. Whether privacy or security requires special arrangements when you communicate with your attorney

CHILDREN

12. The names and birth dates of each child of this marriage, indicating any child who is deceased or of age, and whether or not the wife is pregnant. Also, the address of any minor child who is not residing at home, and the name of the person with whom the child is residing
13. The names and addresses of any persons, other than the parents, who may claim a custodial right to the children
14. The names and ages of any children of the spouses by prior marriage and the name and address of the person who has their custody
15. Any financial obligations to children of a prior marriage
16. Any special needs or disabilities of any of the children
17. The school status of the children and the quality of their performance
18. Any agreed upon or contemplated custodial arrangement and visitation arrangement by the noncustodial parent

19. Any facts or circumstances that cause you serious concern about your spouse's acting as custodian or exercising rights of visitation

20. Children's career or educational goals, if known

INCOME AND PROPERTY

21. The occupation and business address of each spouse

22. The gross salary of each spouse. The take-home pay and whether each spouse receives a commission or income from some other source, with identification of the source

23. Whether the spouses have been filing joint income tax returns, and whether either files returns other than personal returns, such as partnership or corporate returns

24. Whether either party is contemplating an employment change in the foreseeable future, and how that will affect income

25. The employability of a spouse, if unemployed

26. A description of any checking and savings accounts maintained by the parties, the balances, named titleholders to the accounts, and the sources of deposits

27. A description of any securities owned by the parties, current market value, named titleholder, date of purchase, and source of purchase money

28. Location of any stock certificates and whether any substantial sales have been made in preceding months

29. A description of any real estate owned by the parties, purchase price, current market value, mortgage balance, monthly payments, including taxes and insurance, date of purchase, source of purchase money, and your preference regarding disposition of particular parcels of real estate

30. A list of personal property, including household furnishings, automobiles and other vehicles, boats, and jewelry; valuations where available and desired disposition

31. A description of any safe-deposit boxes maintained by the spouses and the contents thereof

32. A description of any insurance policies maintained by the spouses. The beneficiaries and the death benefits of life insurance. Name of any health and accident insurer

33. A description of any monies due either spouse and a list of outstanding debts other than monthly utilities

34. A description of any gifts or inheritance anticipated by either spouse or their children

35. Any financial obligations to a spouse of a former marriage

SPECIFIC MARITAL PROBLEMS

36. A description of the cause and duration of any marital separations during the entire marriage period

37. The spouses' history of marital counseling, if any

38. The spouses' history of psychological counseling, if caused by other than domestic problems

39. History of mental, physical, or sexual abuse by the spouse or other member of the household that poses a present threat to any member of the household, if any

40. Whether either of the spouses has previously filed suit for divorce or separate maintenance, or consulted lawyers in connection with problems of this marriage

41. Discussions, if any, the parties have had about separation or divorce

42. The actions or omissions of the other spouse that cause the client to seek legal advice at this time

43. Alternatives, if any, the parties have considered or discussed other than separation or divorce

44. Specific misconduct of the spouse that would constitute grounds for divorce or would be the basis for special relief in terms of support, property division, child custody, or domestic violence protection

RELIEF REQUESTED

45. The current financial needs of the parties and their children in the form of a budget and any change in those needs contemplated in the near future

46. Client's expectations and preferences regarding the division of property in the event of a divorce

47. Immediate needs in terms of support, housing, debt assistance, injunctive relief, physical protection, or custody and support of the children

48. Whether threat of domestic violence or abuse requires application for an Order of Protection

49. Long-range support needs of either spouse

50. Intentions regarding remarriage and employment

51. Spouses' present plans to relocate residence

52. Whether the wife wishes to resume her maiden name in the event of divorce

53. Problems in the home, between the spouses, or with the children that require immediate attention through professional counseling

ATTORNEY RETAINER AGREEMENT—SAMPLE

September 9, 1996

Mr. John Doe
Chicago, Illinois

Re: Retainer Agreement

Dear Mr. Doe:

Thank you for selecting our firm to represent you in your dissolution action. This letter sets forth the retainer agreement concerning our firm's representation of you and shall become effective when we receive a signed copy from you.

Our representation will include advising, counseling, negotiating, investigating, and handling this family law matter to final settlement or adjudication. Every effort will be made to handle your case promptly and efficiently according to the highest legal and ethical standards. We shall attempt to keep you informed as to the progress of your case at all stages. Services will be rendered on your behalf by me as well as Estelle P. Nameher on an as needed basis. Our paralegals will be in charge of document handling and a variety of important tasks that do not require the services of an attorney. I will be principally responsible for negotiation, trial, and overall supervision of your file. Our billable hourly rates effective January 1, 1996, are as follows:

Name	Office, Deposition, and Routine Court Motions	Trials and Contested Court Motions
John T. Namehim	$200	$250
Estelle P. Nameher	120	140
Paralegals	50	

To the extent that any other partners or associates perform services on your behalf, they will bill at their regular hourly rate. No change in our billing rates will be made without advance notification to you.

Mr. John Doe
September 9, 1996
Page Two

Your retainer fee is $3,500, against which time and costs will be charged as they are incurred at our normal hourly rates. Due to the varied nature of family law cases and the possibility of unforeseen circumstances, it is impossible to quote a specific total fee for legal services. You are principally responsible for all of your attorneys' fees. Should you seek to terminate your action for any reason, any balance due in excess of the retainer will be payable at that time.

You will be billed for all time spent in handling your case, which includes, but is not limited to, consultation and meeting time, telephone and correspondence, court proceedings, including waiting time and travel time, research, preparation of documents, discovery, including depositions, interrogatories, production and inspection of documents, and general preparation and negotiation for any of the above. Your bill will reflect the particular service rendered and the individual rendering the service. Time is recorded in tenths of an hour.

You are responsible for all costs, which include but are not limited to Court fees, accounting or expert fees, stenographer fees, copy costs, and facsimile transmissions. While we expect prompt payment upon billing, if your cash flow needs require you to spread or defer your payments for a reasonable period of time, please contact me to make appropriate arrangements. We do expect costs advanced by us to be reimbursed promptly. If you have any questions regarding a particular billing, we ask that you call it to my attention before the next month's statement is due.

The foregoing represents the substance of our retainer agreement. If you have any questions, please contact me or feel free to review this proposed agreement with another attorney. If the terms of our retention are acceptable to you, please so indicate by signing the enclosed copy of this letter and returning same to me.

Very truly yours,

John T. Namehim

JTN/psh
Enclosure

I have read the above retainer agreement and accept its terms.

Dated: _____   _____

John Doe

CHILD SUPPORT GUIDELINES—SAMPLES

CALIFORNIA

Statewide uniform guidelines for determining child support

(a) The statewide uniform guideline for determining child support orders is as follows: $CS = K [HN - (H\%) (TN)]$.

(b)(1) The components of the formula are as follows:

(A) CS = child support amount.

(B) K = amount of both parents' income to be allocated for child support as set forth in paragraph (3).

(C) HN = high earner's net monthly disposable income.

(D) $H\%$ = approximate percentage of time that the high earner has or will have primary physical responsibility for the children compared to the other parent. In cases in which parents have different time-sharing arrangements for different children, $H\%$ equals the average of the approximate percentages of time the high earner parent spends with each child.

(E) TN = total net monthly disposable income of both parties.

(2) To compute net disposable income, see Section 4059.

(3) K (amount of both parents' income allocated for child support) equals one plus $H\%$ (if $H\%$ is less than or equal to 50 percent) or two minus $H\%$ (if $H\%$ is greater than 50 percent) times the following fraction:

Total Net Disposable Income Per Month	K
$0–800	$0.20 + TN/16{,}000$
$801–6,666	0.25
$6,667–10,000	$0.10 + 1{,}000/TN$
Over $10,000	$0.12 + 800/TN$

For example, if $H\%$ equals 20 percent and the total monthly net disposable income of the parents is \$1,000, $K = (1 + 0.20) \times 0.25$, or 0.30. If $H\%$ equals

80 percent and the total monthly net disposable income of the parents is $1,000, K = (2 − 0.80) × 0.25, or 0.30.

(4) For more than one child, multiply CS by:

2 children	1.6
3 children	2
4 children	2.3
5 children	2.5
6 children	2.625
7 children	2.75
8 children	2.813
9 children	2.844
10 children	2.86

(5) If the amount calculated under the formula results in a positive number, the higher earner shall pay that amount to the lower earner. If the amount calculated under the formula results in a negative number, the lower earner shall pay the absolute value of that amount to the higher earner.

(6) In any default proceeding where proof is by affidavit pursuant to Section 2336, or in any proceeding for child support in which a party fails to appear after being duly noticed, H% shall be set at zero in the formula if the noncustodial parent is the higher earner or at 100 if the custodial parent is the higher earner, where there is no evidence presented demonstrating the percentage of time that the noncustodial parent has primary physical responsibility for the children.

(7) In all cases in which the net disposable income per month of the obligor is less than one thousand dollars ($1,000), the court shall rule on whether a low-income adjustment shall be made. The ruling shall be based on the facts presented to the court, the principles provided in Section 4053, and the impact of the contemplated adjustment on the respective net incomes of the obligor and the obligee. Where the court has ruled that a low-income adjustment shall be made, the child support amount otherwise determined under this section shall be reduced by an amount that is no greater than the amount calculated by multiplying the child support amount otherwise determined under this section by a fraction, the numerator of which is 1,000 minus the obligor's net disposable income per month, and the denominator of which is 1,000. If a low-income adjustment is allowed, the court shall state the reasons supporting the adjustment in writing or on the record and shall document the amount of the adjustment and the underlying facts and circumstances.

ILLINOIS

The court may order either or both parents owing a duty of support to a child of the marriage to pay an amount reasonable and necessary for his support, without regard to marital misconduct. The duty of support owed to a minor child includes the obligation to provide for the reasonable and necessary physical, mental, and emotional health needs of the child.

(1) The Court shall determine the minimum amount of support by using the following guidelines:

Number of Children	Percent of Supporting Party's Net Income
1	20
2	25
3	32
4	40
5	45
6 or more	50

(2) The above guidelines shall be applied in each case unless the court makes a finding that application of the guidelines would be inappropriate, after considering the best interests of the child in light of evidence including but not limited to one or more of the following relevant factors:

(a) the financial resources of the child;

(b) the financial resources and needs of the custodial parent;

(c) the standard of living the child would have enjoyed had the marriage not been dissolved;

(d) the physical and emotional condition of the child, and his educational needs; and

(e) the financial resources and needs of the non-custodial parent.

NEW YORK

Parents' duty to support child

1. (a) Except as provided in subdivision two of this section, the parents of a child under the age of twenty-one years are chargeable with the support of such child and, if possessed of sufficient means or able to earn such means, shall be required to pay for child support a fair and reasonable sum as the court may determine. The court shall make its award for child support pursuant to the provisions of this subdivision. The court may vary from the

amount of the basic child support obligation determined pursuant to paragraph (c) of this subdivision only in accordance with paragraph (f) of this subdivision.

(b) For purposes of this subdivision, the following definitions shall be used:

(1) "Basic child support obligation" shall mean the sum derived by adding the amounts determined by the application of subparagraphs two and three of paragraph (c) of this subdivision except as increased pursuant to subparagraphs four, five, six and seven of such paragraph.

(2) "Child support" shall mean a sum to be paid pursuant to court order or decree by either or both parents or pursuant to a valid agreement between the parties for care, maintenance and education of any unemancipated child under the age of twenty-one years.

(3) "Child support percentage" shall mean:

(i) seventeen percent of the combined parental income for one child;

(ii) twenty-five percent of the combined parental income for two children;

(iii) twenty-nine percent of the combined parental income for three children;

(iv) thirty-one percent of the combined parental income for four children; and

(v) no less than thirty-five percent of the combined parental income for five or more children.

(4) "Combined parental income" shall mean the sum of the income of both parents. . . .

(f) The court shall calculate the basic child support obligation, and the non-custodial parent's pro rata share of the basic child support obligation. Unless the court finds that the non-custodial parent's [FN1] pro-rata share of the basic child support obligation is unjust or inappropriate, which finding shall be based upon consideration of the following factors:

(1) The financial resources of the custodial and non-custodial parent, and those of the child;

(2) The physical and emotional health of the child and his/her special needs and aptitudes;

(3) The standard of living the child would have enjoyed had the marriage or household not been dissolved;

(4) The tax consequences to the parties;

(5) The non-monetary contributions that the parents will make toward the care and well-being of the child;

(6) The educational needs of either parent;

(7) A determination that the gross income of one parent is substantially less than the other parent's gross income;

(8) The needs of the children of the non-custodial parent for whom the non-custodial parent is providing support who are not subject to the instant action and whose support has not been deducted from income pursuant to subclause (D) of clause (vii) of subparagraph five of paragraph (b) of this subdivision, and the financial resources of any person obligated to support such children, provided, however, that this factor may apply only if the resources available to support such children are less than the resources available to support the children who are subject to the instant action;

(9) Provided that the child is not on public assistance (i) extraordinary expenses incurred by the non-custodial parent in exercising visitation, or (ii) expenses incurred by the non-custodial parent in extended visitation provided that the custodial parent's expenses are substantially reduced as a result thereof; and

(10) Any other factors the court determines are relevant in each case,

the court shall order the non-custodial parent to pay his or her pro rata share of the basic child support obligation, and may order the non-custodial parent to pay an amount pursuant to paragraph (e) of this subdivision.

JOINT PARENTING AGREEMENT—SAMPLE
(BOTH PARENTS EMPLOYED)

The following is submitted to the Court by agreement of the husband, JOHN DOE ("JOHN"), and the wife, MARY DOE ("MARY"), herein as an agreed plan for the sharing of custodial and child care responsibilities of their minor children, NANCY and THOMAS. The parties have entered into this agreement freely and voluntarily in order to serve the best interests of their children. The terms of the parties' agreed plan, which will be incorporated in a subsequent Judgment for Dissolution of Marriage, are as follows:

Principal Residence

1. While both parents are fit and proper parents to administer the care, custody, control, and education of their minor children, the parties agree to share their legal custody jointly and to maintain the children's place of principal residence with MARY.

General Purpose

2. JOHN and MARY acknowledge that NANCY and THOMAS will have a continuing need for frequent contact with both parents in order to minimize the effects of the termination of their marriage upon them. The parties further acknowledge that their circumstances and the children's circumstances may change over the period of time this Agreement is in effect. They have, therefore, specified herein certain methods of resolving disputes, and modifying the terms hereof as necessary.

3. Both parents have the expressed desire to minimize the disruption of the children's lifestyle, normal emotional growth, and successful development in the environment within which they are to be raised. To that end, the parties agree:

A. That each parent will endeavor to foster the love and respect of the children for the other parent. Neither parent shall speak disparagingly of the other parent or their families in the presence of NANCY or THOMAS.

B. The children's need for security, a sense of home and neighborhood ties, established schedules for school, extracurricular activities, traditional family gatherings and special events will not be disregarded by either parent, and both parents will endeavor to maintain these important elements in each child's life.

Information Sharing

4. Both parents shall actively participate in raising and guiding the children and to that end will share pertinent information in connection with their physical, medical, dental, and psychological needs as well as their education and progress in school. Medical and school records for the children will be made available to both parents, and each of them shall be notified of consultations and invited to confer with teachers, counselors, or medical professionals concerning each child's education and health care.

Decision Making

5. Both parents acknowledge that in matters of major concern, including, but not limited to, education, medical care, attendance at camp and extracurricular activities, the parties will consult with each other and make every reasonable effort to reach vital decisions jointly. Each parent shall apprise the other of the necessity of making such a vital decision when the need arises while a child is in his or her physical care. In case of emergency, the parent with physical care of the child shall take whatever emergency action is necessary to meet the health care or other need. As soon as possible thereafter, the parent making such an emergency decision will advise the other parent of same.

Religious Training

6. The parties agree that they will be jointly responsible for the children's religious instruction and any costs in connection therewith. Both parents will cooperate to see that the children attend scheduled services and instruction classes in the **Nameit faith,** and both shall be free to participate in their religious activities whenever appropriate.

Day Care

7. The parties agree that it is in the children's best interest to have **Jane Nameher** continue to serve as their primary sitter. Each party shall have telephone access to the children at any reasonable time when they are with the other parent or the sitter. The sitter's services shall be made available to either parent when the children are staying at that parent's home.

Modification and Enforcement

8. Either party who wishes to modify this Agreement shall submit a proposed letter or other writing concerning such modification to the other parent, and the parties shall consult prior to any action being taken in accordance with paragraph 9.

9. If the parents cannot agree on a vital decision affecting the welfare of the children, the Circuit Court of **Nameit County** shall retain continuing juris-

diction to adjudicate any disputed issue. The parties agree by this order, however, to submit any such disputed issue for resolution by an impartial mediator, mutually agreed upon, before applying to the Court for relief. If the parties cannot agree to the mediator, each party shall name a mediator who shall select a third mediator. In case of emergency or if the mediation is unsuccessful, a Court proceeding may be filed by either party. The parties agree to share equally the cost of the mediator, whether or not the mediation is successful.

Removal of Residence

10. The parties agree that geographic proximity is necessary to accomplish the goals of their Joint Parenting Agreement. Therefore, neither party will permanently remove the residence of the children from the State of Illinois without the written agreement of the other or permission of the Court, based upon the best interest and welfare of NANCY and THOMAS.

Parenting Time

11. The time spent by each parent with the children is set forth on Exhibit A attached. In connection with the exercise of visitation generally, the parties shall abide by the following rules:

A. Provide at least 24 hours advance notice if he or she is unable to exercise a visitation right.

B. Telephone the other parent as soon as practicable if he or she will be more than 30 minutes late.

C. Pick up and return the children promptly to the agreed place of pickup and return. JOHN will provide the transportation when he picks up and returns the children, and he may participate in transporting them to or from school after prior notice to MARY.

D. Contact the other parent as early as practicable of any scheduling conflict or illness that will make either child unavailable.

E. Have the children appropriately dressed and ready at the time they are due to be picked up or returned.

F. Take all reasonable steps to avoid scheduling events or activities for either child during scheduled visitation times.

G. Should a child have unavoidable activities which conflict with the visitation schedule, the parent with whom the child is residing at the time shall take him or her to those activities and may participate in same if appropriate.

H. Give the other parent notice and the option to care for the children when that parent will be away from home for 48 hours or more.

I. Each parent shall inform the other in advance of any extended out-of-town trips with a child, including details of location, duration, and a telephone number, if available.

Support

(Support provisions are optional in the Parenting Agreements. You may prefer to place them elsewhere in the Judgment.)

12. Based on JOHN's net monthly income of MORE$ and MARY's net monthly income of LESS$, JOHN will pay MARY the sum of $_____ per month for the support of each child, payable on the first day of each month commencing **DATE.**

13. Each parent shall be solely responsible for providing necessary support and living expenses for the children when they are with that parent, including the cost of the sitter.

14. Each parent shall pay for a child's travel costs when the child is traveling with that parent.

15. JOHN and MARY shall continue to maintain their current health insurance coverage for the children or any substituted coverage. MARY shall pay one-third of any ordinary medical or dental expenses for a child which are not covered by insurance, and JOHN shall pay two-thirds of such expenses.

Education Expense

16. JOHN shall pay two-thirds and MARY shall pay one-third of each child's tuition expense at the preschool and the parochial school they currently attend. Should a child attend another private institution, the parties will share the tuition costs on the same basis or as agreed upon by them at the time. The cost of any private tutoring recommended by a child's teacher will be shared on the same basis.

17. Each of the parents shall contribute to a child's college (or graduate school) expenses in amounts commensurate with their respective incomes and financial abilities at the time. The existence of custodial or trust funds established for the benefit of a child's education shall be taken into account before allocating the parents' financial responsibilities in connection with higher education.

_____

JOHN DOE

_____

MARY DOE

EXHIBIT A

JOHN's regular parenting time with NANCY and THOMAS shall currently be as follows:

1. Regular Parenting Time

From Friday evening at dinnertime until Sunday evening at 5:00 P.M. on alternate weekends and every Tuesday and Thursday from 5:00 P.M. to 7:00 P.M. (or 8:30 P.M. if the next day is a school holiday). For purposes of this schedule the foregoing shall pertain to weekends.

A. Holiday time or extended time shall take precedence over the regular weekend sequence.

B. When a parent has extended parenting time for seven days or more, the other parent will have the weekend preceding and the weekend following the extended period or such portion thereof which is available.

C. Notwithstanding the regular weekend schedule, the children shall be available to either parent to celebrate significant family events, including parent birthday celebrations, and for dinner and limited visits when the other parent is absent.

2. Holiday Parenting Time

A. The children shall follow the regular weekend sequence on Easter holiday except that both parents may attend the Easter Sunday service at their church.

B. Mother's Day and MARY's birthday shall be spent with MARY.

C. Father's Day and JOHN's birthday shall be spent with JOHN.

D. Each child's birthday celebration shall be shared by the parents.

E. The parents shall alternate the following holidays: Memorial Day, Independence Day, Labor Day, Thanksgiving (including Friday and the weekend), New Year's Eve through New Year's Day.

G. When a holiday falls on a Monday, the parent entitled to visitation shall have the preceding weekend as well.

3. Extended Parenting Time

A. The first half of Christmas vacation from the Sunday after school lets out until 1:00 P.M. Christmas Day shall be spent with JOHN in even numbered years and with MARY in odd numbered years. The balance of the Christmas vacation shall be spent with the other parent.

B. The children shall spend the first half of their spring vacation with their father from Friday when school lets out until Wednesday afternoon and the balance of the spring vacation with their mother. Once THOMAS is 10 years old, the parents shall alternate spring vacations.

C. The children shall have summer visitation with JOHN for two consecutive weeks or more at times to be agreed upon by the parents. MARY shall also be entitled to an extended summer vacation with the children. JOHN shall have preference in selecting his summer vacation period in even numbered years, and MARY shall have preference in odd numbered years, if the selection is made before May 1. Regular visitation is suspended during the other parent's extended visitation period.

PRETRIAL MEMORANDUM—SAMPLE

IN THE CIRCUIT COURT OF _____ COUNTY, _____
COUNTY DEPARTMENT, DOMESTIC RELATIONS DIVISION

IN RE THE MARRIAGE OF:

)
)   NO.
)
)
)   CALENDAR: _____
)
)
)
)
)

_____
PETITIONER

       AND

_____
RESPONDENT

PRE-TRIAL MEMORANDUM

A pre-trial memorandum is to be prepared by each attorney of record. Failure to prepare a pre-trial memorandum shall be considered a violation of rules and result in appropriate sanctions.

Schedules A and C shall be filed with the pre-trial judge seven (7) days prior to the initial pre-trial conference.

Schedule B shall be filed with the judge to whom the case is assigned before the date set for the mediation intake session.

The _____ Petitioner _____ Respondent _____ Attorney for Child _____ Other presents the following information.

All items are to be filled in.

NAME: _____

ADDRESS: _____

DATE OF BIRTH: _____

SS#: _____

CONDITION OF HEALTH (SPECIFY) CONDITION:

_____

_____

EDUCATIONAL BACKGROUND:

_____

_____

DATE OF MARRIAGE: _____

DATE OF SEPARATION: _____

CHILDREN:

NAME   AGE   DATE OF BIRTH

_____

_____

_____

_____

_____

_____

GROUNDS: (Specify party alleging grounds:)

_____

SUMMARY OF DISPUTED ISSUES: (CHECK DISPUTED ISSUES. ISSUES NOT CHECKED WILL BE DEEMED UNDISPUTED.)

____ Dissolution	____ Dissipation		
____ Legal Separation	____ Value of property		
____ Declaration of Invalidity	____ Amount of Income ____H ____W		
____ Custody/Custody Modification	____ Whether property is marital or non-marital		
____ Visitation	____ Division of marital property		
____ Removal	____ Reimbursement		
____ Child Support/Support Modification	____ Disposition of debts		
____ Maintenance	____ Division of personal property		
____ Educational Expenses	____ Attorney's Fees		

Briefly describe other issues to be resolved:

_____

_____

_____

Prepared by:
ATTORNEY'S NAME AND ADDRESS

SCHEDULE A
COMPARATIVE BALANCE SHEET
JOHN AND MARY DOE

TITLE[1]	MARITAL ASSETS (same as "community")	HUSBAND'S[2] VALUE	WIFE'S VALUE
	BANK ACCOUNTS		
H	First National Bank checking account #123456	Nominal	$ 1,000
W	First Suburban Bank checking account #1234	$ 500	Nominal
	REAL ESTATE		
JT	Residence 123 West Elm St.	200,000	130,000
H	Condo apt. 3912, North State St.	60,000	80,000
	BUSINESS INTERESTS		
H	Dental practice	50,000	200,000
W	Mary Doe Resale Shop	100,000	5,000
	SECURITIES AND SAVINGS		
JT	Barney Smith brokerage, account #98765432	25,750	25,750
W	First Federal money market, account #1234567	10,239	Non-marital[3]
	RETIREMENT FUNDS		
H	IRA First National Bank	12,526	12,526
W	IRA Suburban Bank	4,550	4,550
H	Pension—Dental practice	60,000	100,000
	AUTOMOBILES		
H	1994 Toyota Supra	15,000	25,000
W	1995 Ford Wagon	25,000	15,000

[1] Titleholder indicated by "H" = husband, "W" = wife, "JT" = joint tenancy.

[2] The separate columns indicate each party's position as to the value of an asset or liability. Parties tend to undervalue property they expect to receive and overvalue property their spouses will receive. If the value differences are not compromised, an appraiser may have to be hired. The cost of appraisers and the lack of other evidence of value causes most people to compromise by trial time.

[3] Indicates the wife or husband is disputing the classification of a particular asset as marital or nonmarital.

TITLE	MARITAL ASSETS CONT'D	HUSBAND'S VALUE	WIFE'S VALUE
	PERSONAL PROPERTY		
JT	Furniture and furnishings	100,000	Nominal
JT	Artwork	Non-marital	50,000
W	Jewelry	50,000	Non-marital
H	Jewelry	Nominal	10,000
	OTHER ASSETS		
H	Dissipation	0	100,000[4]
	TOTAL ASSETS:	**$713,565**	**$758,826**
	LIABILITIES		
JT	Mortgage, Elm Street	$ 65,000	$ 65,000
H	Mortgage, condo	45,000	45,000
H	Car loan, Toyota	20,000	20,000
W	Car loan, Ford	15,000	15,000
W	Mastercard	1,500	1,500
H	American Express	3,500	3,500
JT	Elm Street real estate tax, 1996	4,200	4,200
H	Attorney fee balance	5,000	5,000
W	Attorney fee balance	5,000	6,500
	TOTAL LIABILITIES:	**$164,200**	**$165,700**
	NET MARITAL ESTATE	**$549,365**	**$593,126**

[4]Explanatory footnotes are important if the comparative balance sheet is properly prepared. In this case, the wife claims $100,000 in marital dissipation for a bad investment. While acknowledging the loss, the husband claims zero dissipation because he invested in good faith.

TITLE	NON-MARITAL ASSETS (same as "separate")	HUSBAND'S VALUE	WIFE'S VALUE
	Pre-Marital property		
H	Artwork	$5,000	Marital[3]
	Inherited property		
W	1st Federal money market, account #1234567	Marital	$10,239
	Gifted property		
W	Jewelry	Marital	10,000
	TOTAL	$ 5,000	$20,239
W	Loan — Mary Doe Resale Shop	$ 7,500	Marital
	HUSBAND'S NET NON-MARITAL CLAIM	$ 5,000	$ 0
	WIFE'S NET NON-MARITAL CLAIM	$(7,500)	$20,239

SCHEDULE B
INCOME AND EXPENSE AFFIDAVIT
JOHN AND MARY DOE

IN THE CIRCUIT COURT OF _____ COUNTY, _____
COUNTY DEPARTMENT, DOMESTIC RELATIONS DIVISION

IN RE THE MARRIAGE OF:)
)
)
)
_____)
PETITIONER   )
        AND   ) No.
)
) Calendar
_____)
RESPONDENT   )

Actual Monthly
as of

_____

A. STATEMENT OF INCOME AND DEDUCTIONS

1. Gross Income Per Month
   a. Salary/wages $_____
   b. Commissions   _____
   c. Draw   _____
   d. Bonus   _____

   Money in Lieu of Earnings   _____
   e. Pension   _____
   f. Social Security   _____
   g. Public Assistance   _____
   h. Workers' Compensation   _____
   i. Unemployment   _____
   j. Disability Payments   _____

   Investments   _____
   k. Dividends   _____
   l. Interest   _____
   m. Trusts   _____
   n. Rents   _____
   o. Bonds   _____
   p. Annuity   _____

q. Other (specify) _____

_____   _____

TOTAL GROSS MONTHLY INCOME $ _____

  2. Required Deductions
     a. Taxes: Federal (based on ____ exemptions) $ _____
     b. Taxes: State (based on ____ exemptions)   _____
     c. Social Security (or pension ____ equivalent)   _____
     d. Mandatory retirement contributions required
        by law or as a condition of employment   _____
     e. Union Dues   _____
     f. Health/Hospitalization Insurance   _____
     g. Prior obligation of support actually paid
        pursuant to court order   _____
     h. Expenditures for repayment of debts representing
        reasonable and necessary expenses for the
        production of income   _____
     i. Medical expenditures necessary to preserve life
        or health   _____
     j. Reasonable expenditures for the benefit of the
        child and the other parent exclusive of gifts
        (for non-custodial parent only)   _____

TOTAL REQUIRED DEDUCTIONS FROM INCOME   _____

NET MONTHLY INCOME

B. CASH OR CASH EQUIVALENTS ON HAND
  1. Savings and interest-bearing accounts   _____
  2. Checking   _____
  3. Money Market Funds   _____
  4. Mutual Funds   _____
  5. Stocks and bonds   _____
  6. Other (specify) _____

_____   _____

TOTAL CASH OR CASH EQUIVALENT ON HAND   _____

C. STATEMENT OF MONTHLY LIVING EXPENSES
  I. Housing:
     Rent/Mortgage   _____
     Real estate taxes   _____
     Insurance   _____
     Assessments   _____

Condo fees   _____

Homeowner's association   _____

Other   _____

SUBTOTAL HOUSING EXPENSES $ _____

Utilities:

Heat (gas/electric/oil)   _____

Electricity   _____

Telephone   _____

Water   _____

Refuse   _____

Cable TV   _____

SUBTOTAL UTILITY EXPENSES $ _____

Maintenance:

Household help   _____

Yard/snow plowing   _____

Home/yard improvements   _____

Window washer   _____

Appliance and house service contracts   _____

Large appliance replacement   _____

Small item replacement (towels, dishes)   _____

Exterminator   _____

Repairs   _____

Decorating   _____

Cleaning (drapes, gutters)   _____

Other   _____

SUBTOTAL MAINTENANCE EXPENSES $ _____

II. **Food:**

Groceries   _____

Restaurants   _____

SUBTOTAL FOOD EXPENSES $ _____

III. **Transportation Expenses:**

Payments   _____

Gas/oil   _____

Insurance   _____

License/stickers   _____

Repairs   _____

Car wash   _____

Alternate transportation   _____

SUBTOTAL TRANSPORTATION EXPENSES $ _____

IV. **Personal:**
    Clothing   _____
    Grooming   _____
    Dry cleaning/laundry   _____
    Medical: Doctor   _____
                   Dentist   _____
                   Eyes   _____
                   Medication   _____
    Insurance: Life   _____
                   Health   _____
    Entertainment/social obligations _____
    Recreation/vacations   _____
    Donations   _____
    Newspapers/magazines   _____
    Clubs/organizations   _____
    Gifts   _____
    Miscellaneous items   _____
    Other   _____

SUBTOTAL PERSONAL EXPENSES $ _____

V. **Children:** (No: ____ , ages _____)
    Clothing   _____
    Grooming   _____
    Dry cleaning/laundry   _____
    Medical: Doctor   _____
                   Dentist   _____
                   Eyes   _____
                   Medication   _____
    Insurance: Life   _____
                   Health   _____
    Education: Tuition   _____
                   Books/fees/supplies _____
                   School activities   _____
                   Uniforms   _____
                   Transportation   _____
                   Tutoring/lessons   _____
                   Lunches   _____
                   Religious school   _____
                   Other   _____
    Baby-sitter   _____
    Nursery school   _____
    Day care   _____

Allowance   _____
Birthday parties/gifts   _____
Lessons/activities   _____
Books/magazines   _____
Day camp   _____
Overnight camp   _____
Vacations   _____
Other   _____

SUBTOTAL CHILDREN EXPENSES $ _____

VI. **Other Fixed Monthly Expenses:**
Pets (veterinarian/food)   _____
Investments   _____
Retirement plans   _____
Pension funds   _____
Loans   _____
Installment payments   _____
Charge cards (monthly payments)   _____

**SUBTOTAL OTHER FIXED MONTHLY
EXPENSES** $ _____

RECAPITULATION

   I. Housing $ _____
      Utilities   _____
      Maintenance   _____
  II. Food   _____
 III. Transportation   _____
 IV. Personal   _____
  V. Children   _____
 VI. Other Fixed Monthly Expenses   _____

TOTAL EXPENSES $ _____

Net Monthly Income   _____
Less: Expenses   _____
Difference   _____

Under penalties as provided by law in 735 ILCS 5/1-109 of the Code of Civil Procedure, I certify that the statements set forth in this instrument are true and correct.

                                      _____

SCHEDULE C
CUSTODY, VISITATION, AND CHILD SUPPORT

This Schedule was prepared by   [ ] Petitioner   [ ] Respondent
                                  [ ] Attorney for Child   [ ] Other

Child's Name	Sex	DOB	School and Grade	Special Problems

2. Current order in effect relating to custody, visitation, and child support.

3. Present medical policies covering children. (Specify company and how obtained):

4. Professional Examinations and Reports. Unless objected to by specific motion, include the following information: name and type of profession or agency, date, purpose of examination and findings. Reports, if not protected by confidentiality, shall be presented to the pre-trial judge for pre-trial purposes only and shall not be a part of the court file unless otherwise ordered.

5. Other court proceedings having a bearing on custody, visitation, and support. (Name of case, type of action, and last order).

WITNESS'S GUIDE TO THE RULES OF EVIDENCE

The rules of evidence that control the conduct of court hearings and, to a lesser degree, depositions, are extremely complex and vary slightly from state to state. The following simplified guide is designed to give you an overview so that you have at least some idea what is going on at your deposition or trial. Once you get a feeling for these rules, don't be upset if your lawyer doesn't object to every leading question or hearsay answer. Good trial technique suggests that the attorney object only to what may damage your case and not to every harmless error. The hearing will pass much more quickly as a result, and you will avoid irritating the judge with needless objections.

1. *Purpose*: While laypeople often object to the apparent straitjacket that the rules of evidence put on their testimony, the actual purpose of the rules is to provide a system for speedy and fair trials. The rules require evidence to be presented in a manner best designed to determine the truth.

2. *Burden of proof*: The spouse who is seeking any particular relief from the court has the obligation of pleading allegations which justify that relief and then coming forward with testimony or other evidence that will persuade the court that his or her allegations are more probably true than not. If you fail to sustain your burden of proof on an issue, the court finds against you. You lose.

3. *Character evidence*: Inevitably, people in divorce or custody litigation want to bring their friends and relatives to testify as character witnesses. As a general rule, character evidence is not admissible in divorce proceedings to prove that a spouse did or did not engage in a particular course of conduct. Neither is it admissible to prove that John is a "good guy" and Mary is a "bad guy," so John should win. Where a witness's reputation for truthfulness has been attacked, some jurisdictions do allow a limited type of character testimony as to the witness's prior reputation for truthfulness or untruthfulness. This type of testimony is rarely seen in divorce court.

4. *Personal knowledge*: As a general rule, witnesses other than experts testify from their own knowledge—their personal observations. Opinions or interpretations of what you observed will not be required, or allowed, in most cases. The judge will render his or her own opinion on the evidence in making the final determination.

5. *Expert witnesses*: Individuals who have specialized knowledge about some factual issue involved in your lawsuit may testify to assist the court in un-

derstanding the evidence and reaching a final determination. Experts may testify from personal observation, from data examined before the trial, from facts presented at the trial, and from their special knowledge and training. Psychologists, psychiatrists, appraisers, economists, and social workers are some of the experts who are frequently called to testify in matrimonial cases. While they will testify as to their expert opinion on an issue, the court considers that opinion only with the other evidence and is not bound to accept it.

6. *Foundation:* Before certain evidence will be accepted by the court, a preliminary "foundation" must be established. For example, the foundation for a conversation will require preliminary evidence as to when and where the conversation took place, and who was present. The foundation for a photograph will require testimony from a person familiar with the scene or object being photographed, indicating when the photograph was taken and whether it is a fair and accurate representation of the scene being photographed. The purpose of the various foundation requirements is to assure the court that the evidence being offered is true and accurate.

7. *Refreshing recollection:* When a witness is testifying and has exhausted her or his memory regarding a particular event or transaction, the witness may refer to a written document to refresh the recollection. Having inspected the document, the witness then resumes testifying. If the document is a memorandum that was made by the witness at the time of a particular occurrence and records details of the occurrence, it may be admitted in evidence if the witness's recollection is incomplete. If the document was made later on, or was not prepared by the witness, it may be used only to refresh an exhausted memory. Documents and lists prepared for trial may be used in this manner, but once they are used, they are subject to examination by the other side and may be referred to on cross-examination. Your use of documents to refresh your recollection on the witness stand should be arranged with your attorney beforehand as part of your trial preparation. You don't sneak a peek at these documents, you refer to them only with the permission of the court.

8. *Objections:* Where rules of evidence are being violated, this fact is called to the attention of the court by either counsel, who makes an objection to the question being asked or the answer given. The court also has the right to make objections, but the witness may *never* make an objection. If the objection is to the question, the attorney waits until the question is completed and then orally makes the objection and states the reason for it. The court will either sustain (allow) the objection or overrule it. In the latter case, the witness proceeds to answer the question. If the particulars of the question have been forgotten, the witness may ask the court reporter or the attorney to repeat it. If a question has been asked and answered without objection, then any possible objection is waived and the testimony becomes part of the record. The following is a summary of the most common objections that you are likely to hear.

OBJECTIONS TO THE FORM OF THE QUESTIONS

A. *Leading:* On direct examination, the questioner should not suggest the answer in the question, with the result that the witness need only answer "yes" or "no." Instead of saying, "Did you deposit $10,000 in your joint savings account on January 15, 1990?" the questioner should ask whether the witness deposited any money in the savings account, when, and how much. That way the witness is testifying and not the lawyer, and the court is able to measure the credibility of the witness. In order to save time it is generally acceptable to ask leading questions on preliminary information and to assist a witness who has exhausted his or her recollection. Leading questions in crucial factual areas will not be allowed if objection is made. Of course, once a leading question has been made and objected to, it is a simple matter for the attorney to rephrase the question in proper form, and the witness will know the information being sought. If this is done repeatedly, the questioner may be reprimanded by the court. In any event, the credibility of the testimony will be undermined if a witness is constantly led.

B. *Compound question:* A question containing two or more questions is confusing to the witness, and any attempted answer may confuse the court. The attorney should ask only one question at a time. The same is true of questions that are ambiguous or not clearly phrased. If an objection is made, the court will ask counsel to rephrase the question.

C. *Lack of foundation:* If the questioner seeks to elicit certain testimony or the admission of documentary evidence that requires a preliminary foundation, the court will sustain an objection to its admission until the foundation is properly laid by the required series of questions.

D. *Presumption of facts not in evidence:* Where the questioner includes in the question facts or presumptions that are not in evidence or that are in dispute, the question is objectionable. "When did you first start beating your wife?" or "What did you do to stop your wife's overspending?" are objectionable unless the beating or overspending is undisputed. The answer will be confusing because it will not be clear whether the witness is admitting the presumed facts. This type of manipulative question will frequently confuse or anger the witness who is not able to catch the presumption and correct it before answering the rest of the question. The same is true where the questioner misquotes the witness's testimony on direct examination in a cross-examination question. The question should be objected to and the quotation corrected before any answer is given. You should be wary of any cross-examination questions that tend to put words in your mouth, especially if the words taste unfamiliar.

E. *Argumentative:* Questions that are intended to persuade the judge rather than elicit information, or that call for an argument from the witness, are objectionable. The questioner frequently tips off an argumentative implication by beginning the question with a phrase such as "In other words" or "Would you have this court believe?" If the argumentative question is not objected to, the witness is better off answering "yes" or "no," if that is possible, rather than arguing back.

F. *Repetitive:* The witness need not answer the same question over and over again, even if the form of the question is slightly changed each time. One answer on each point is enough, and repetition is usually done on cross-examination for purposes of harassment or to elicit slight differences in the multiple answers so as to create discrepancies that may undermine the witness's credibility.

OBJECTIONS TO ANSWERS

A. *Unresponsive:* If the witness's answer goes off the subject of the question, the questioner can object to the answer as being unresponsive and ask that the answer be stricken from the record.

B. *Narrative answers:* On direct examination, questions should be specific. If the question is so broad it requires a long narrative answer, the opposing attorney will not be able to anticipate objectionable testimony. Once the inadmissible testimony has been spoken, the objection may well be too late. Therefore, the attorney has the right to object to broad questions before they are answered. The question "Can you tell us how your husband treated you last year?" is too broad, and if objection is made, the court will require the attorney to rephrase the question, directing it to some particular conduct or particular time that is relevant to the subject in issue.

C. *Opinion and speculation:* Where the witness is interpreting the evidence by giving personal opinions or speculation, the answer may be stricken from the record. Neither can the witness *characterize* conduct by calling it "wonderful," "negligent," "good," or "evil," or by using other adjectives that inject editorial opinion into the events being described.

OBJECTIONS TO CONTENT OF QUESTION OR ANSWER

A. *Irrelevant:* Evidence is relevant if it tends to prove or disprove some matter that is at issue in your case. If it is not relevant, the court does not want to hear it because it does not aid in the determination of the case. In matrimonial cases, clients have a tendency to want to litigate many issues that ventilate their feelings as to who is the "good guy" and who is the "bad guy" in their marriage, and they are disappointed when the court refuses to admit such testimony. The primary difference between a skilled lawyer and a layperson in matters of litigation is a trained sense of relevancy. What is emotionally most important to you may be irrelevant to the court.

B. *Hearsay:* You cannot testify to the verbal or written statement someone made, unless your spouse was present. This is one of the most widely known — and widely misunderstood — rules of evidence because of its many exceptions. For your purposes as a witness, it is enough to know that you or your witnesses cannot testify about what Betty, John, or Bob said if your spouse was not present to hear it. The reason for the rule is the lack of opportunity to cross-examine Betty, John, or Bob to determine whether any of them really made the alleged statement and whether what they said was true. On the other hand, if in preparing for trial, you have evidence that may appear to be hearsay, don't discard it. Call it to your attorney's attention, and you may find that it is not hearsay after all, or that it is admissible as an exception. It is also not a bad idea to prepare certain hearsay testimony; though it may not be admissible on your direct examination, it may be sprung on the opposition in response to a careless question on cross-examination.

C. *Exceed scope of direct examination:* The cross-examiner raises questions relative only to the subject matter contained in the direct testimony and cannot bring up new matter unless it is done in the attempt to undermine the credibility of the witness. If the opposing lawyer wishes to open new areas of inquiry with the witness, he or she must wait and recall the witness when putting on his or her own case.

TRIAL OUTLINE: GROUNDS
(FAULT STATES ONLY)—SAMPLE

I. *Introduction*
  A. Name, address, age, length of residence in the jurisdiction
  B. Date and place of marriage; number of children born or adopted to this marriage; children by prior marriages living in home
  C. Employment of witness and spouse

II. *Conduct of witness as a spouse*
  A. Activities as homemaker or breadwinner, or both
  B. Contribution toward child care
  C. Any other evidence that witness was a dutiful spouse

III. *Grounds—misconduct of other spouse*
  A. *Option 1*: Relate events *chronologically*, for example:
    1. Late Dec. 1988: Relate physical cruelty act that required medical treatment.
    2. 1990–1997: Relate series of lesser acts, including physical and mental cruelty, that have more significance as a *course* of cruel conduct, presuming no single act is of great magnitude, e.g., pushing, shaking, poking with finger, some of which is done in front of friends, along with vile or abusive language, so as to cause humiliation. Add evidence of other misconduct, such as increasing lack of affection, staying out late at night without explanation, dissipation of income and assets, nagging, unjustified criticism, et cetera, as they occurred in a given time period.
  B. *Option 2*: Relate events *categorically*, for example:
    1. Relate all acts of physical cruelty from 1988 to present.
    2. Relate all examples of belittling or demeaning conduct in front of third parties from 1988 to present.
    3. Relate examples of late hours, lack of affection, et cetera, from 1988 to present.
  C. *Option 3*: Combine *categorical and chronological*, for example:
    1. Relate physical and mental cruelty by category during 1988 to next significant time period, e.g., 1994, when the youngest child entered school.

    2. Relate acts of physical and mental cruelty by category from 1992 to next significant time period, then to present.

D. After relating events, detail conduct or event that led to final separation. It is best if evidence leads to an apparent crisis so that a continuation of the marriage relationship appears impossible, or at least unreasonable:

    1. Add testimony that plaintiff did not cause or provoke any of the misconduct by the spouse (if necessary to counterdefense of provocation).

    2. Add testimony that plaintiff has lived separate and apart as a single person without fault.

E. Note in preparing your trial outline:

    1. Each incident or category of misconduct should be given a separate subheading, number, or letter so that your attorney can select those incidents that have most impact as evidence and eliminate irrelevant or minor evidence that may water down the overall presentation. Selected incidents may be moved around in the outline for more effective presentation.

    2. The most is not always the best. You may want to include *everything* in your outline, not realizing that some incidents make you look worse than your spouse. Let your attorney determine the strategy and select the events that will lead to the most effective presentation of your case.

    3. The stronger your grounds, the shorter your outline, for example:

        a. On January 1 we were married.

        b. On January 2 he hit me with a hammer.

        c. On January 3 he stabbed me with a sword.

        d. We separated on January 3 and have remained apart.

        e. I did not provoke the bludgeoning or stabbing.

          End of outline—end of case.

Unfortunately—or fortunately—everyone can't have such a strong case. The outline, in any case, is a useful tool—both to teach you what is relevant and to familiarize your attorney with the facts of your particular case. It puts you both on the same wavelength for the trial. Trial judges appreciate thorough preparation and lose patience with both witnesses and attorneys who appear not to have organized and rehearsed their presentations.

TRIAL OUTLINE: PROPERTY
AND SUPPORT—SAMPLE

I. *Introduction*

Name, address, years of marriage, number of children, present employment of self and spouse (may be omitted if the judge is already aware of this information from earlier hearings on this case)

II. *Income of Spouses*

A. Present evidence of current gross income and take-home pay of self and spouse, if you know.

B. Note any improper or excessive deductions, e.g., has five children but claims no exemptions.

C. Note any trends in employment history of self or spouse, e.g., steady increase or decline; sudden decline coinciding with filing of divorce suit; opportunity for additional income from tips, expense account overtime, or bonus; incidence of unrecorded income from cash payments, moonlighting, or payment in kind, e.g., spouse does mechanic's bookkeeping in exchange for car repair.

D. Note employment benefits and "executive compensation," e.g., free insurance, use of country club, automobile, air transportation, paid vacations.

E. Note any deferred benefits from employers, e.g., pension or profit-sharing plans, bonuses, delayed salary increase, deferred commissions.

III. *Property of Spouses*

A. List all property of spouses, with valuations (if agreed). Disputed items will require present market-value testimony from a qualified witness or appraiser.

B. Property list prepared in writing in advance of trial in balance sheet or similar form should be presented to opposing counsel for comment as to accuracy. Trial can be limited to disputed items, with a list of agreed property items offered in evidence by agreement.

C. In community or equitable distribution jurisdictions, community or marital property should be separated from individual property. The latter is generally not subject to division by the court, but may affect the amount of the marital estate each spouse is awarded. For disputed items evidence must provide:

1. Time and source of original acquisition
2. History of any transfers, tracing original asset to its present form
3. Any prior agreements of spouses as to disposition
4. Statement as to whether there was any commingling of title or ownership between spouses
5. Financial contribution to acquisition and maintenance of property, including contribution as a homemaker

D. In common-law property states evidence must prove:
1. Title to property
2. Special equities from prior agreements or financial contribution

IV. *Need of spouse and children for support*
   A. Establish family's standard of living through past activities and expenditures.
   B. Establish current living costs by written budget, which may be in affidavit form (see Income and Expense Affidavit, p. 189), indicating both actual and estimated monthly expenses. If amounts come from checkbook summary, standard of living may be established at the same time.
   C. Any special needs anticipated in the near future should also be presented to the court so that they can be worked into the current budget, e.g., eyeglasses, orthodontia, monthly payments on a new car, furnace, roof, et cetera.
   D. If other spouse is in the habit of making substantial expenditures for things such as clothing, club memberships, sports equipment, entertainment, this may be offered as proof of both a high standard of living and financial ability beyond apparent means.

V. *Advise court how special needs require a particular division of marital property: e.g., home and furniture for children, savings needed for business capital, car needed to get to work.*

VI. *Other problems or support issues.*

TRIAL OUTLINE: CHILD CUSTODY—SAMPLE

The following trial outline is designed for the parties themselves or witnesses who are going to describe their personal observations regarding custody issues. This outline is not for *expert* witnesses.

I. *Identification and background*
  A. Age; education; employment
  B. Relationship to child; opportunity to observe child or parents, or both

II. *Description of each child*
  A. Age; mental and physical health; elaborate on any special problems
  B. Progress in school; grades; best and worst subjects; teacher comments (report cards); absenteeism and tardiness; school activities; awards; discipline; elaborate on any special achievements or problems
  C. Child's relationship with others:
    1. Siblings (effects of separating children)
    2. Playmates (general sociability, special friends; effect of change of environment; ability to make new friends)
    3. Adults (response to authority; teachers, coaches; relatives; neighbors)
    4. Parents or parent figures (affection shown to and from child in relation to each; responsiveness to discipline; comments, complaints, or expressed preference of child toward each; nature and regularity of activities with each)

III. *Physical description of present or future home*
  A. Residence: Rooms; bedroom for child; furnishings; cleanliness; other household members. Is this where child will live?
  B. Neighborhood: Physical condition of homes; proximity of friends, parks, transportation, school; incidence of crime, or other negative or positive factors

IV. *Description of each parent or potential custodian*
  A. Witness's relationship to parent (if witness is not the parent)
  B. Each parent's background, e.g., age, mental and physical health, education, employment (history of employment can be included if it demonstrates instability or special training, et cetera)

C. Parents' past relationship with child in terms of nurturing, disciplining, regular activities

D. Any significant changes in a parent's relationship with child in terms of nature of activities or time spent with child

E. Factors that favor *either* parent as potential custodian, e.g., education, training, or experience; priorities as they affect children; stability of personality, environment, or career; past history as principal nurturing parent; certainty, predictability, or discernibility of future environment and conduct as they may affect children; personal commitment to children's welfare; ability to provide alternate supervision or home care when necessary; availability of supportive family and friends to provide secure home atmosphere.

F. Factors that undermine either parent's fitness as potential custodian:

1. Prior misconduct or bad habits that have actual or potential effect on children's moral, emotional, or physical welfare

2. Demonstrated inability to meet children's everyday nurturing needs, e.g., cooking, cleaning, affection, discipline, willingness or ability to be there when children need something or to provide suitable alternate supervision and home care

3. Statements or conduct that suggests children's welfare is secondary priority, e.g., statements or threats in part that suggest that custody effort has ulterior motive, such as spite, leverage on other issues, or a *need* for the children, rather than the reverse; a demonstrated willingness to frequently leave the children alone or with others in order to voluntarily pursue activities that are personally gratifying; repeated attempts to involve children in marital problems, e.g., pressing for their support, efforts to belittle or downgrade the other parent in children's eyes; past indifference to necessary professional checkups or treatment for children; a dramatic change in attitude toward children from indifference to fixation that coincides with the matrimonial litigation

4. Demonstrated or diagnosed mental or emotional illness or instability that is likely to affect parenting ability

V. *Conclusion*

A. Witness's opinion as to custodial arrangement that will serve children's best welfare and reasons for that opinion. (In some jurisdictions only an expert witness can be asked for such an opinion.)

B. Based on witness's observation and knowledge, what harm would witness foresee if children were placed with the other parent?

QUALIFIED DOMESTIC RELATIONS ORDER—SAMPLE

IN THE CIRCUIT COURT OF NAMEIT COUNTY

IN RE THE MARRIAGE OF:	)
	)
MARY DOE,	)
Petitioner,	)
	)
and	) No.
	)
JOHN DOE,	)
Respondent.	)

QUALIFIED DOMESTIC RELATIONS ORDER

THIS MATTER coming before this Court for the purpose of entry of a Qualified Domestic Relations Order under the Retirement Equity Act of 1984, all parties having been given property notice and having agreed to the form and substance of this Order, and the Court being fully advised in the premises;

THE COURT FINDS AS FOLLOWS:

A. On __DATE__ the Court entered a Judgment for Dissolution of Marriage (hereafter referred to as "Judgment") in the above entitled case, dissolving the marriage of the parties.

B. The Judgment provides, in part, for the division of marital property, the sum of $150,000 from JOHN DOE's interest in the NAMEIT International Employees Savings and Defined Contribution Plan (referred to as "the Plan"). This Order is applicable to that Plan.

C. Specifically, the Judgment contains the following provision in reference to the division of the Plan:

"The sum of $150,000.00 to be transferred pursuant to a Qualified Domestic Relations Order to the Wife, at her direction, from the Husband's interests in the NAMEIT 401(k) Plan."

D. No portion of any benefits under the Plan are required to be paid to any other alternate payee under any other Qualified Domestic Relations Order and no such order has ever been entered.

E. The address of MARY DOE, hereinafter referred to as "the Alternate Payee" under this Order, is MARY'S ADDRESS . Her Social Security Number is 123-45-6789.

F. The address of JOHN DOE, hereinafter referred to as "the Participant" under this Order, is JOHN'S ADDRESS . His Social Security Number is 123-45-6789.

IT IS HEREBY ORDERED AS FOLLOWS:

1. The Alternate Payee shall be entitled to a distribution of $150,000.00, plus any appreciation, interest, and/or dividends accrued on this amount since September 20, 1995, from the Plan.

2. To the extent allowable under the terms and provisions of the Plan, the Alternate Payee's interest shall be distributed to her in a lump sum; in a form which will allow her to roll over said sum into a qualified individual retirement account or plan in her name alone, or any other form which will allow the Alternate Payee to liquidate said funds.

3. Payments to the Alternate Payee shall commence as soon as administratively possible under the Plan. The Alternate Payee shall have the right to elect any options available to the Participant under the Plan at any time, including any lump-sum distribution available.

4. The Participant shall forthwith execute or cause to be executed such documents or do such acts as are necessary to give the Alternate Payee the right to her interest in the Plan, as more fully described in paragraph 1 above and to any benefits payable to a surviving spouse.

5. Nothing in this Order requires and the Order shall not be construed to require the Plan to provide any type or form of benefit or any option not otherwise provided under said Plan.

6. The parties intend this Order to qualify as a Qualified Domestic Relations Order pursuant to the Internal Revenue Code of 1954 and the Employee Retirement Security Act of 1974, both as amended by the Retirement Equity Act of 1984, and that it will be interpreted and administered as such.

7. This Court shall retain jurisdiction to supervise the payment of benefits herein and to amend this Order for the purpose of establishing or maintaining this Order as a Qualified Domestic Relations Order. The Court may amend this Order to effectuate the express provisions of this Order, the Judgment for Dissolution of Marriage and any modification to said Judgment.

8. A copy of this Order shall be promptly submitted by counsel for the Alternate Payee to the Plan Administrator.

APPROVED:

_____
Attorney for Petitioner

ENTER:_____

JUDGE

_____
Attorney for Respondent

DATED:_____

QUALIFIED MEDICAL CHILD
SUPPORT ORDER—SAMPLE

IN THE CIRCUIT COURT OF NAMEIT COUNTY
COUNTY DEPARTMENT—DOMESTIC RELATIONS DIVISION

IN RE THE MARRIAGE OF	)	
	)	
MARY DOE,	)	
Petitioner,	)	
	)	
and	)	No. _____ D _____
	)	
JOHN DOE,	)	
Respondent.	)	

QUALIFIED MEDICAL CHILD SUPPORT ORDER

This court having entered a judgment of dissolution of marriage on the same date as the entry of this Order, and the court being otherwise fully advised in the premises;

IT IS HEREBY ORDERED AND ADJUDGED:

1. This Order is intended to serve as a Qualified Medical Child Support Order ("QMCSO") which orders the Medical Plan specified below to provide medical benefits to the children of Petitioner, MARY DOE, and Respondent, JOHN DOE, who are named below ("Alternate Recipients"), pursuant to a Judgment of Dissolution of even date herewith, and in accordance with Section 609 and other relevant sections of the Employee Retirement Income Security Act of 1974, as amended ("ERISA"), and Section 505.2 of the Illinois Marriage and Dissolution of Marriage Act.

2. The Medical Plan subject to this Order is as follows:
"Medical Plan for the Employees of NAMEIT INTERNATIONAL," or successor plans.
Plan Administrator:
    a. Name: _____
    b. Address: _____

3. The Participant is the Respondent, JOHN DOE, whose last known address, Social Security Number, and date of birth are: _____

_____

4. The Petitioner is MARY DOE, whose last known address, Social Security Number, and date of birth are: _____

_____

5. The Alternate Recipients, their last known addresses, Social Security Numbers, dates of birth, and custodial parent(s) are:

I. Nancy Doe: _____

_____

II. Thomas Doe: _____

_____

6. The Petitioner and the Respondent were married on __**DATE**__ and their marriage was dissolved on the date of this Order.

7. The Alternate Recipients shall receive the following benefits under the Medical Plan:

[Family medical and dental coverage/family medical coverage/medical coverage under the _____ option presently available under the Medical Plan/coverage in the HMO]

Other: _____

If the Medical Plan is changed so that the Medical Benefits specified in this paragraph are no longer available, the medical benefits provided shall be the family medical coverage, taking into account the extent of coverage, coinsurance amount, and deductible (if applicable) that is most similar to the coverage specified; however, such benefits shall be benefits that are permitted under the Medical Plan, or its successor.

8. The period to which this Order applies shall be from the date of the entry of this Order to the first to occur of the youngest surviving Alternate Recipient completing his or her education or reaching his or her 23rd birthday.

9. The Petitioner, MARY DOE, having been awarded residential custody of each of the Alternate Recipients pursuant to ERISA § 609, is deemed to have been appointed by each of the Alternate Recipients to receive copies of notices sent to each Alternate Recipient with respect to this Order.

10. Any payment of medical benefits made pursuant to this Order in reimbursement of expenses paid by an Alternate Recipient or an Alternate Recipient's custodial parent shall be made to the Alternate Recipient or the Alternate Recipient's residential custodial parent, MARY DOE, as applicable.

11. This Order does not require the Medical Plan to provide any type or form of benefit, or any option, not otherwise provided under the Medical Plan.

12(i). It is intended by the parties that this Order will qualify as a Qualified Medical Child Support Order pursuant to ERISA Section 609 (29 U.S.C.A. § 1169), and subsequent amendments, and that it will be interpreted and administered as such.

12(ii). The Court retains jurisdiction to amend this Order for the purpose of establishing or maintaining this Order as a Qualified Medical Child Support Order; and, further, the Court may amend this Order to revise or conform its terms so as to effect the expressed provisions of the Order, the parties' Settlement Agreement dated _____ , 199__, and the Judgment of Dissolution of Marriage, as well as to enforce this Order against successor medical insurance plans, to provide coverage for a child who moves out of the service area, or to modify this Order to comply with the requirements of ERISA Section 609 (29 U.S.C.A. § 1169).

_____

MARY DOE

_____

JOHN DOE

_____

NAMEHIM
Attorney for Petitioner

_____

NAMEHER
Attorney for Respondent

ENTER:

_____

JUDGE

ORDER OF PROTECTION—SAMPLE

INTERIM/PLENARY ORDER OF PROTECTION: 1 of 3 Pages

CCG-83-1-20M-12/29/92(31369)

IN THE CIRCUIT COURT OF COOK COUNTY

People ex rel. _____
_____ on behalf of
_____ self and/or behalf of

_____

Petitioner

-vs-

_____

Respondent

Case No. _____

☐ Independent Proceeding

☐ Other Civil Proceeding

   (Specify) _____

☐ Criminal Proceeding

☐ Juvenile Proceeding

LEADS NO. _____

PETITIONER	ADDRESS	CITY
	☐ (Check if omitted pursuant to Statute)	
RESPONDENT	ADDRESS	CITY

Birthdate	Sex	Race	Height	Weight	Hair	Eyes	Social Security Number *(if known)*
(Required for LEADS)							

ORDER OF PROTECTION

4552 ☐ **INTERIM**   **4652** ☐ **PLENARY**

ANY KNOWING VIOLATION OF ANY ORDER OF PROTECTION FORBIDDING PHYSICAL ABUSE, NEGLECT, EXPLOITATION, HARASSMENT, INTIMIDATION, INTERFERENCE WITH PERSONAL LIBERTY, WILLFUL DEPRIVATION, OR ENTERING OR REMAINING PRESENT AT SPECIFIED PLACES WHEN THE PROTECTED PERSON IS PRESENT OR GRANTING EXCLUSIVE POSSESSION OF THE RESIDENCE OR HOUSEHOLD, PROHIBITING ENTERING OR REMAINING AT THE HOUSEHOLD WHILE UNDER THE INFLUENCE OF ALCOHOL OR DRUGS AND SO CONSTITUTING A THREAT TO THE SAFETY AND WELL-BEING OF ANY PROTECTED PERSON, OR GRANTING A STAY AWAY ORDER, IS A CLASS A MISDEMEANOR. GRANT OF EXCLUSIVE POSSESSION OF THE RESIDENCE OR HOUSEHOLD SHALL CONSTITUTE NOTICE FORBIDDING TRESPASS TO LAND. ANY KNOWING VIOLATION OF ANY ORDER AWARDING LEGAL CUSTODY OR PHYSICAL CARE OF A CHILD, OR PROHIBITING REMOVAL OR CONCEALMENT OF A CHILD MAY BE A CLASS 4 FELONY. ANY WILLFUL VIOLATION OF ANY ORDER IS CONTEMPT OF COURT. ANY VIOLATION MAY RESULT IN FINE OR IMPRISONMENT. STALKING IS A FELONY.

(Definitions of prohibited conduct on reverse)

The following persons are protected by this Order: _____
_____

"The minor child/ren" referred to herein are: _____
_____

Date, time and place for further hearing *(if Interim Order)*:

Date _____ Time _____ Courtroom/Calendar No. _____
                                           Location _____

This Order was issued on:	This Order will be in effect until:
Date _____ Time _____	☐ Date _____ Time _____ ☐ Vacated by court order. ☐ Specified event: _____

1.) CLERK OF THE CIRCUIT COURT

BASED ON THE FINDINGS OF THIS COURT, ☐ WHICH WERE MADE ORALLY FOR TRANSCRIPTION, OR ☐ WHICH ARE SET OUT IN A SEPARATE INSTRUMENT FILED WITH THE COURT, AND WITH THE COURT HAVING JURISDICTION OF THE SUBJECT MATTER AND OVER ALL NECESSARY PARTIES, IT IS HEREBY ORDERED THAT:

☐　1.　With respect to all Protected Persons, Respondent is prohibited from committing the following:

　　☐ Physical abuse;　　☐ Harassment;　　☐ Interference with personal liberty;　　☐ Intimidation of a dependent;
　　☐ Willful deprivation;　　☐ Neglect;　　☐ Exploitation;　　☐ Stalking,

☐　2.　Petitioner is granted exclusive possession of the residence and Respondent shall not enter or remain in the household or premises located at:

_____
(This remedy does not affect title to property)

☐　3.　☐ a. Respondent is ordered to stay away from Petitioner and other protected persons; and/or

　　☐ b. Respondent is prohibited from entering or remaining at _____

　　_____ while any Protected Person is present; and/or

　　☐ c. Respondent is allowed access to the residence on (date) _____ at (time) _____ in the presence of
　　(name) _____ to remove items of clothing, personal adornments, medications used exclusively
　　by the Respondent and other items, as follows: _____

☐　4.　Respondent is ordered to undergo counseling at _____

　　for a duration of _____

☐　5.　☐ a. Petitioner is granted physical care and possession of the minor child/ren; and/or

　　☐ b. Respondent is ordered to:

　　　☐ Return the minor child/ren _____ to the physical care of
　　　_____ ; and/or

　　　☐ Not remove the minor child/ren _____ from
　　　the physical care of Petitioner or _____

☐　6.　Petitioner is granted temporary legal custody of the minor child/ren _____

☐　7.　☐ a. Respondent is awarded visitation rights on the following dates and times or under the following conditions or parameters:
　　(No order shall merely refer to the term "reasonable visitation")

　　_____
　　_____

　　☐ b. Respondent's visitation is restricted as follows:

　　_____
　　_____

　　☐ c. Respondent's visitation is denied.

　　(Petitioner may deny Respondent access to the minor child/ren if, when Respondent arrives for visitation, Respondent is under the influence of drugs or alcohol and constitutes a threat to the safety and well-being of Petitioner or Petitioner's minor child/ren or is behaving in a violent or abusive manner.)

☐　8.　Respondent is prohibited from removing the minor child/ren from Illinois or concealing them within Illinois.

☐　9.　Respondent is ordered to appear in Courtroom/Calendar _____ at _____

　　_____ on _____ at _____ AM/PM, with/without the minor child/ren.

☐　10.　Petitioner is granted exclusive possession of the following personal property and the Respondent is ordered to promptly make available to Petitioner said property that is in Respondent's possession or control, to wit:

_____
(This remedy does not affect title to property)

☐　11.　Respondent is prohibited from taking, encumbering, concealing, damaging or otherwise disposing of the following personal property:

_____ , except as explicitly authorized by the Court.

　　☐ Further, Respondent is prohibited from improperly using the financial or other resources of an aged member of the family or household for the profit or advantage of Respondent or any other person.

☐　12.　Respondent is ordered to pay temporary support for ☐ Petitioner and/or ☐ the minor child/ren of the parties as follows:

　　$ _____ per _____ , starting _____ , payable ☐ through the Clerk of the Circuit Court,
　　or ☐ directly to Petitioner.

☐　13.　Respondent is ordered to pay $ _____ as actual monetary compensation for loss(es) to _____

　　on or before _____ .

　　☐ Further, Respondent is ordered to pay court costs in the amount of $ _____ and attorney fees in the amount of $ _____
　　to _____ in connection with any action to obtain, modify, enforce, appeal or
　　reopen any order of protection, on or before _____

1.) CLERK OF THE CIRCUIT COURT　　　　　　　　CASE NO. _____

CCG-83-3-20M-12/29/92(31369)

☐ 14. Respondent is prohibited from entering or remaining at the household or residence located at _____
_____ while under
the influence of alcohol or drugs and so constituting a threat to the safety and well-being of any Protected Person.

☐ 15. Respondent is denied access to school and/or any other records of the minor child/ren and is prohibited from inspecting, obtaining, or
attempting to inspect or obtain such records.

☐ 16. Respondent is ordered to pay $ _____ to the following shelter _____
on or before _____ .

☐ 17. Respondent is further ordered and/or enjoined as follows:
_____
_____

☐ 18. The relief requested in paragraph(s) _____ of the petition is *(DENIED) (RESERVED)*, because:
_____
_____ .

PLENARY ORDERS ONLY

This order shall remain in effect until:

☐ 1. Two years following the date of entry of such Order, such expiration date being _____ , or
such earlier date, as ordered by the Court, such expiration date being _____ .

☐ 2. Final judgment in conjoined proceeding is rendered.

☐ 3. This Order is modified or vacated (provided such Order is incorporated into the final judgment of another civil proceeding).

☐ 4. Termination of any voluntary or involuntary commitment, or until _____ .
(not to exceed 2 years)

☐ 5. Final disposition when a Bond Forfeiture Warrant has issued, or until _____ .
(not to exceed 2 years)

☐ 6. Expiration of any supervision, conditional discharge, probation, periodic imprisonment, parole, or supervised mandatory release,
plus 2 years.

☐ 7. Expiration of a term of imprisonment set by this Court, plus 2 years.

NOTICE: Upon 2 days notice to Petitioner, or such shorter notice as the Court may prescribe, a Respondent subject to an Interim Order of Protection
issued under the IDVA may appear and petition the Court to re-hear the original or amended Petition. Respondent's petition shall be verified and
shall allege lack of notice and a meritorious defense.

Date _____

Judge _____
Judge's No.

Attorney (or Pro Se Petitioner) Name _____

Address _____

City _____

Phone _____

Attorney # _____

Service by Facsimile ☐ will be accepted ☐ will not be accepted.

Facsimile Number _____
(Must be included if service by facsimile is accepted)

CASE NO. _____

1.) CLERK OF THE CIRCUIT COURT

DEPENDENCY EXEMPTION WAIVER—
IRS FORM 8332

Form **8332** (Rev. December 1987) Department of the Treasury Internal Revenue Service	**Release of Claim to Exemption for Child of Divorced or Separated Parents** ▶ **Attach to Tax Return of Parent Claiming Exemption**	OMB No. 1545-0915 Expires 10-31-90 Attachment Sequence No. **51**

Name(s) of parent claiming exemption as shown on tax return | Social security number

Part I   Release of Claim to Exemption for Current Year

I agree not to claim an exemption for _____

                                        Name(s) of child (or children)

for the calendar year 19 _____ .

_____

Signature of parent releasing claim to exemption | Social security number | Date

If you choose not to claim an exemption for this child (or children) for future tax years, complete Part II, as explained in the instructions below.

Part II   Release of Claim to Exemption for Future Years

I agree not to claim an exemption for _____

                                        Name(s) of child (or children)

for tax year(s) _____

                (Specify. See instructions.)

_____

Signature of parent releasing claim to exemption | Social security number | Date

---

Paperwork Reduction Act Notice.— We ask for this information to carry out the Internal Revenue laws of the United States. We need it to ensure that taxpayers are complying with these laws and to allow us to figure and collect the right amount of tax. You are required to give us this information.

Purpose of Form.—This form may be used to release the claim to a child's exemption by a parent who has custody of his or her child and might have been entitled to claim the exemption for this child. This form is completed by the parent who has custody of the child and is given to the parent who will claim the exemption. The parent who will claim the child's exemption must attach this form, or a similar statement, to his or her tax return. See **How To File Form 8332,** below.

Exemption for Child of Divorced or Separated Parents.—In general, the parent who has custody of the child (or children) for the greater part of the year is treated as having provided over half of the child's support for purposes of the dependency exemption for the child if:

1. The child receives over half of his or her support from both of the parents; AND

2. The child was in the custody of one or both of his or her parents for more than half of the year.

This general rule applies to parents who are divorced or legally separated under a decree of divorce or separate maintenance, separated under a

written separation agreement, or who lived apart at all times during the last 6 months of the calendar year.

This general rule does not apply if **any** of the following apply:

(a) The parent having custody signs a written statement agreeing not to claim the child's exemption and the parent not having custody attaches this statement to his or her tax return for the tax year. (See **Parent Who Releases Claim to Exemption,** below.)

(b) The child is treated as having received over half of his or her support from a person under a multiple support agreement (**Form 2120,** Multiple Support Declaration).

(c) A qualified divorce decree or written agreement was in effect before January 1, 1985, and provides that the noncustodial parent can claim the exemption for the child, and the noncustodial parent provides at least $600 for the support of the child during the year.

Note: *If items (b) or (c) above do not apply, the noncustodial parent must attach a completed Form 8332, or similar statement, to his or her tax return for each year in which the noncustodial parent claims the child's exemption.*

Parent Who Releases Claim to Exemption.—A parent who might be entitled to claim the child's (or children's) exemption because of having custody of the child for a greater part of the calendar year may agree to

release claim to the child's exemption for the current calendar year or for future years, or both. The release can be made by completing Form 8332 or a similar statement.

Part I should be completed by the parent who chooses to release claim to the child's (or children's) exemption for the current calendar year.

Part II should be completed by the parent who chooses to release claim to the child's (or children's) exemption for a specified number of future years, or for all future years. If the parent is releasing claim for all future years, "all future years" should be written in the space provided for in Part II.

How To File Form 8332.—The noncustodial parent must attach Form 8332, or a similar statement, to his or her tax return for the tax year in which the noncustodial parent claims the child's exemption. If the parent having custody of the child completes Part II of Form 8332, the noncustodial parent must attach a copy of this form to his or her tax return for each succeeding year in which the noncustodial parent claims the exemption

The parent who receives the release of claim to the child's exemption may claim the exemption **only** if the other tests in the Form 1040 or 1040A Instructions for dependency exemptions are met.

For more information, get **Publication 504,** Tax Information for Divorced or Separated Individuals.

Form **8332** (Rev 12-87)

Sample
Worksheets

ASSET/LIABILITY WORKSHEET

(Provide requested information on separate worksheets in columns under indicated Roman numerals and headings.)

ASSETS

I. *Real Estate*
   Address and Description   Date Acquired   Cost   Value as of (date)   Balance of Mortgage   Titleholder   Use

II. *Savings, CD's, Money market, Treasury bills or notes, Commercial paper*
   Describe Account   Date Acquired   High Balance   Source of Investment   Balance as of (date)

III. *Checking*
   Describe Account   Date Acquired   Balance as of (date)   Average Balance   Titleholder   Used By

IV. Stocks and bonds

Name & Number of Shares	Exchange	Date Acquired	Titleholder	Value as of (date)	Cost	Where Located

V. Closely held corporations

Name and Number or Percent of Ownership	Date Acquired	Titleholder	Date & Amount of Last Sale or Valuation

VI. Partnerships/Joint ventures

Name & Percent of Ownership	Date Acquired	Amount of Investment	Value as of (date)	Add'l. Capital Required	Title	Avg. Annual Income/Loss

VII. Sole Proprietorships

Nature of Business Activity	Date Acquired	Market Value	Avg. Annual Income/Loss

VIII. *Pension and Profit sharing*

Name of Plan	Owner of Interest	Date entered Plan	Vesting Date or Vested Percent	Time & Method of Distrbtn.	Value as of (date)

IX. *Cash-value life insurance (Whole Life)*

Insurance Company	Policy Number	Insured	Beneficiary	Owner	Value as of (date)	Loans	Annual Premium

X. *Patents, Copyrights, Royalties*

Owner	Description of Interest	Date Acquired	Benefits to Date	Value as of (date)

XI. *Vehicles and Boats*

Description	Date Acquired	Titleholder	Cost	Value as of (date)	Loan Balance

XII. *Furnishings, Antiques, Artworks, Collections*
(List household furnishings and appliances by room on schedule to be attached. *Other items of value list below.*)

Description	Date Acquired	Who Acquired	Cost	Source of Payment	Value as of (date)	Where Located

XIII. *Accounts Receivable*

Payable To	Name of Debtor	Balance Due	Manner & Amt. of Payments	Nature of Debt

XIV. *Miscellaneous Assets*

Describe	Date Acquired	By Whom	Cost	Source of Payment	Value as of (date)	Other Considerations

LIABILITIES

XV. *Secured debts and delinquent real estate taxes or assessments*

Creditor	Date and Loan No.	Debtor	Balance as of (date)	Monthly Payments	Describe security and name of any co-signer

XVI. *Unsecured debts and income taxes due*

Creditor	Date Incurred	By Whom	Balance as of (date)	Monthly Payment

XVII. *Contingent debts:*

Creditor	Basis for Claim	When Debt Accrued	Date & Amount Due	Describe Contingencies

INSURANCE WORKSHEET

Locate all policies if possible and list them below.

I. Life Insurance:

Insurer and Policy Number	Term or Whole Life	Insured	Owner	Beneficiary	Premium	Death Benefit	Loans	Net Cash Value

II. Home or renters' insurance: (Fire, Liability, and Extended Coverage)

Insurer and Policy Number	Expiration Date	Premium	Named Insured	Agent's Phone No.

III. Auto or boat:

Insurer and Policy Number	Expiration Date	Premium	Named Insured	Vehicles Covered	Agent's Phone No.

IV. Health, accident, or major medical:

Insurer and Policy Number	Expiration Date	Persons Covered	Premium	Claims Procedure	Agent's Phone No.

V. Other insurance:

Company and Policy Number	Type of Insurance	Expiration Date	Premium	Beneficiary

GLOSSARY

The words in this glossary are defined as they are most commonly used in connection with divorce cases.

ACTION   (Same as Cause of Action.) The legal term for what is commonly called a lawsuit.

AFFIDAVIT   A written statement of facts made under oath and signed before a notary public or other officer who has authority to administer oaths.

AFFIRMATIVE DEFENSE   New facts or legal defenses in response to the spouse's pleading constitute a legal defense, even if the allegations of the complaint were true; a bar to legal relief.

AGREEMENT   The oral or written resolution of disputed issues that is incorporated into a court order, judgment, or decree.

ALIMONY   Spousal support. Same as maintenance.

ALIMONY IN GROSS   Spousal support in a single payment or fixed total sum in periodic installments. Sometimes called lump-sum alimony.

ALLEGATION   Statement of facts contained in a pleading, setting forth what the pleader intends to prove.

ALTERNATE PAYEE   The spouse receiving retirement benefits as a result of being married to the individual who was employed and participated in the retirement plan.

APPEAL   The process whereby a higher court reviews the proceedings in a lower court and determines whether there was reversible error. If so, the appellate court amends the judgment or remands the case to the lower court for a new trial.

APPEARANCE   The formal submission by a defendant to the jurisdiction of the court after having been served a summons or knowing that the complaint has been filed. Appearance also refers to the physical presence of a party at a court hearing.

BIFURCATION   The trial of a case in two parts. In the first part the question of grounds for divorce is heard. If the grounds are established, the second part consists of the trial on issues involving property division, alimony, child support, custody, or attorneys' fees.

CHANGE OF VENUE   A change of judges before whom the case is to be tried, requested by a party to the action who feels that the original judge is prejudiced.

CLAIM   A charge by one spouse against the other.

COMMUNITY PROPERTY   All income and property (regardless of who holds title) acquired by the spouses during the course of their marriage, with the exception of property acquired by inheritance or gift. The manner of division differs among community property states, but the tendency is toward equal division. (See *joint property*.)

COMPLAINT   The initial pleading in an action for divorce, separate maintenance, or annulment, setting forth the allegations upon which the requested relief is based. Called a petition in some states.

CONDONATION   The misconduct of a spouse is no longer grounds for divorce if the complaining party appears to forgive it by, for example, continuing to cohabit with the offender.

CONTEMPT OF COURT   The willful failure to comply with a court order, judgment, or decree by a party to the action. Also, any willful act by a person, whether or not a party to the action, that interferes with the court proceeding or somehow contravenes the authority or dignity of the court. Contempt of Court is punishable by fine or imprisonment.

CONTESTED CASE   Any case where the court must decide one or more issues that are not agreed to by the parties. All cases are considered contested until all issues have been agreed to.

COST BASIS   The cost of real estate or investment property consisting of the purchase price plus the cost of capital improvements. This combined sum subtracted from the sale price computes the capital gain or loss for tax purposes.

COUNT   A statement of facts in a pleading constituting the pleader's case or cause of action. A pleading may contain one or more counts, e.g., a count for divorce and a count for legal separation. In some cases the counts are pleaded separately, and in others they are combined.

COUNTERCLAIM   A pleading filed by the defendant, making claims against the plaintiff.

COURT ORDER   The court's written ruling. See *order*.

CROSS-EXAMINATION   The questioning of a witness presented by the opposing party on trial or at a deposition. The purpose is to test the truth of that testimony or to develop it further.

DECREE   The final ruling of the judge on an action for divorce, legal separation, or annulment. Same as judgment.

DEFAULT ORDER OR DEFAULT JUDGMENT   An order or judgment given by the court without the other side's being heard because they failed to plead within the time allowed or failed to appear at the hearing.

DEFENDANT   The one who defends the lawsuit brought by another. Same as respondent.

DEPOSITION   The testimony of a witness taken out of court under oath and reduced to writing. The most common depositions are discovery depositions taken for the purpose of discovering the facts upon which a party's claim is based or discovering the substance of a witness's testimony before trial. The deposition may be used to discredit a witness if he or she changes testimony. Evidence depositions are used to preserve the testimony of a witness who will be unable to appear at trial.

DIRECT EXAMINATION   The initial questioning of a witness by the attorney who called the witness to the stand.

DISCOVERY   Procedures followed by attorneys in order to determine the nature, scope, and credibility of the opposing party's claim. Discovery procedures include depositions, written interrogatories, and notices to produce various documentation relating to issues that are decided in the case. Psychological examinations and court social service investigations are also part of discovery.

DISCRETION OF THE COURT   The area of choice available to a judge to make a legally acceptable decision on his or her interpretation of the evidence.

EMANCIPATION   The point at which a minor child comes of age. Children are emancipated in most states upon reaching the age of either eighteen or twenty-one, or upon marriage, full-time employment, or entering the armed services. Emancipation terminates the duty to support unless a state's statutes require support for the disabled or for educational purposes, i.e., high school or college.

EQUITABLE DIVISION OF PROPERTY   A system of dividing property acquired by spouses during their marriage in connection with a divorce proceeding. The division is based on a variety of equitable factors, including relative financial contribution, contribution as a homemaker, and respective need. Title to property in the name of either spouse does not necessarily restrict the court's right to award that property to the other spouse as part of an equitable division.

EVIDENCE   Documents, testimony, or other demonstrative material offered to the court to prove or disprove allegations in the pleadings.

EX PARTE   The application for court relief without the presence of the other party, because of either a lack of notice or the choice of the other party not to appear.

FOUNDATION   The evidence that must be presented before asking certain questions or offering documentary evidence on trial. See the Witness's Guide to the Rules of Evidence, page 195.

GROUNDS FOR DIVORCE   The legal circumstances that must be proved before a divorce can be granted. Only Illinois and South Dakota currently require proof of marital misconduct. The other states require proof of incompatibility, irretrievable breakdown of the marriage, or separation for a specified minimum period.

HEARING   Any proceeding before the court where testimony is taken or arguments offered by the attorneys for the purpose of resolving disputed issues.

HOLD-HARMLESS   When one spouse assumes liability for a debt or obligation and promises to protect the other from any loss or expense in connection therewith.

HOSTILE WITNESS   A witness who demonstrates so much prejudice during direct examination that the party who has called the witness is allowed to cross-examine. The greater flexibility of cross-examination enables the questioner to ask leading questions and to attack the creditability of the hostile witness. See the Witness's Guide to the Rules of Evidence, page 195.

IMPEACHMENT   The act of proving either by prior inconsistent statement or other conflicting evidence that a witness is lying.

INDEMNIFICATION   To promise to reimburse another person in case of an anticipated loss; the same as hold-harmless.

INJUNCTION   A court order forbidding someone from doing a particular act that is likely to cause physical or mental injury or property loss to another party.

INTERLOCUTORY DECREE   A judgment of the court that is not final until the passage of a certain period of time. During the interlocutory period the parties cannot remarry.

INTERROGATORIES   A series of written questions served upon the opposing party in order to discover certain facts regarding the disputed issues in a matrimonial proceeding. The answers to interrogatories must be under oath and filed within a prescribed period of time.

JOINT PROPERTY   Property held in the name of more than one person. (See *community property* and *marital property*.)

JUDGMENT   The order of the court on a disputed issue; same as decree.

JURISDICTION   The power of the court to rule upon issues relating to the parties, their children, or their property.

LEGAL SEPARATION   A cause of action for support while the spouses are living separate and apart; in many states this is called separate maintenance. Actions for legal separation provide for maintenance, child custody, and support but generally do not provide for division of property. A decree of legal separation does not dissolve the marriage and does not allow the parties to remarry.

LEVERAGE FACTORS   Particular considerations, based on the priorities of the parties, that induce them to settle disputed issues. The skillful employment of these factors generally controls the outcome of a settlement.

LUMP-SUM ALIMONY   Spousal support in a single payment or fixed total sum paid in periodic installments. Sometimes called alimony in gross.

MAINTENANCE   Spousal support; same as alimony.

MARITAL PROPERTY   Accumulated income and property acquired by the spouses during the marriage, subject to equitable distribution by the court. States will vary on their precise definition of what is to be included in marital property, sometimes excepting property acquired by gift or inheritance. (See *community property* and *joint property*.)

MISTRIAL   A trial that is terminated before its completion, as the result of the occurrence of some fundamental error that would render the trial invalid. Following a mistrial, the case must be tried again from the beginning.

MOTION   A written or oral application to the court for some particular relief, such as temporary support, injunction, or attorneys' fees.

NO-FAULT DIVORCE   A marriage dissolution system whereby divorce is granted without the necessity of proving one of the parties guilty of marital misconduct.

NONMARITAL PROPERTY   The term given to property owned before the marriage or acquired during the marriage by gift or inheritance in some equitable distribution states. The same as separate property.

ORDER   The court's ruling on a disputed issue requiring the parties to do certain things or setting forth their rights and responsibilities. The order is reduced to writing and may be signed by the judge and filed with the court by agreement, without necessity of a court hearing.

ORDER OF PROTECTION   State courts provide broad injunctive protection to abused, threatened, harassed, or exploited individuals, their children, and their property by issuing Orders of Protection against the abuser. Petitions for Orders of Protection can be filed in civil or criminal courts. Violations of these orders can be prosecuted as crimes in criminal court or as contempt of the civil court.

PARENS PATRIAE   A doctrine whereby the state will take jurisdiction over any minor children living within its borders. This doctrine is the basis upon which certain states will assume jurisdiction in child custody disputes, even though a divorce action was decided or is pending in another state.

PERSONAL JURISDICTION   The power of the court to order a spouse to do a particular thing, such as pay alimony or child support.

PETITION   A written application for particular relief from the court. In some jurisdictions complaint for divorce is entitled "petition for dissolution." Some jurisdictions require that petitions be sworn and that the petitioners state under oath that the allegations contained in the petition are true.

PLAINTIFF   The party who files the lawsuit. Same as petitioner.

PLAN PARTICIPANT   The employed spouse who participates in the retirement benefits plan that is subject to division by a Qualified Domestic Relations Order upon divorce.

PLEADING   Formal written application to the court for relief and the written response thereto. Pleadings include complaints, answers, petitions, responses, motions, and all counterpleadings.

PRAYER   That portion of a pleading, usually at the end, which specifies the *relief* requested of the court.

PRIVILEGE   The right of a spouse to make admissions to an attorney, clergyperson, or psychiatrist that are not later admissible in evidence.

QDRO   This stands for Qualified Domestic Relations Order, the means provided under federal law (ERISA) to divide retirement benefits between spouses involved in a domestic relations (marriage dissolution, support, or separation) proceeding.

QMCSO   This stands for Qualified Medical Child Support Order, the means provided under federal law to require group health insurance companies to provide health coverage for the children of an insured parent going through a divorce.

REBUTTAL   The introduction of evidence at a trial that is in response to new matter raised by the defendant at an earlier stage of the trial.

RELIEF   Whatever a party to a lawsuit asks the court to do: dissolve the marriage, award support, enforce a prior court order or decree, divide property, enjoin certain behavior, dismiss the complaint of the other party, and so on.

RELOCATION   The term used to describe cases where the custodial parent seeks court permission to move the residence of a minor child from the state where the divorce or last custody order was entered. Also referred to as removal cases.

RESPONSE   The pleading filed in answer to the allegations of a petition. The response may also allege affirmative defenses to those allegations.

RULES OF EVIDENCE   The rules that govern the method of presentation and admissibility of oral and documentary evidence at court hearings or depositions.

SEPARATE MAINTENANCE   A cause of action for support in cases where the spouses live in separate households; same as legal separation.

SEPARATE PROPERTY   The term given to property owned before the marriage or acquired during the marriage by gift or inheritance in community property and some equitable distribution states. The same as nonmarital property.

SETOFF   A debt or financial obligation of one spouse that is deducted by the court from the debt or financial obligation of the other.

SETTLEMENT   The agreed resolution of disputed issues.

SETTLEMENT AGREEMENT   The settlement reduced to a written document.

SHOW CAUSE   (Same as Rule to Show Cause.) A contempt of court proceeding to enforce court orders, judgments, or decrees that have been violated. The alleged violator is given an opportunity to show cause why he or she should not be held in contempt or to comply with the court order. Failing both of these, the court may find the violator in contempt of court and may enter sanctions in the form of fine or imprisonment. The latter is a last resort, where all other efforts at compliance with the court order have failed.

SPECIAL EQUITY   A special interest in property arising from the agreement of the parties or some special contribution toward the acquisition or preservation of the property.

STATUS QUO   The existing state of things; leaving things as they are without modification or alteration. "Things" can be anything from visitation arrangements to property rights.

STIPULATION   An agreement between the parties or their counsel, usually relating to matters of procedure.

SUBPOENA   A document served upon a person who is not a party to the action, requiring him or her to appear and give testimony at a deposition or court hearing. A subpoena is normally accompanied by a witness fee set by statute, as well as a mileage fee for transportation costs to and from the place to which the individual is subpoenaed. Failure to comply with the subpoena could result in punishment by the court.

SUMMONS   A written notification to the defendant that an action has been commenced against him or her and requiring that the defendant appear within a specified period of time to answer the complaint.

SURREBUTTAL   Testimony offered by the defendant to counter any new matter contained in the rebuttal testimony offered by the plaintiff.

TEMPORARY MOTIONS   Application to the court for interim relief pending the final decree of divorce, separate maintenance, or annulment. Typical temporary motions include motions for temporary alimony, child support, attorneys' fees, custody, visitation, enforcement, or modification of prior temporary orders. The court enters a temporary order after hearing a temporary motion.

TESTIMONY   Statements under oath by a witness in a court hearing or deposition.

TRIAL   A formal court hearing to decide disputed issues raised by the pleadings.

VACATED   When a court order, judgment, or decree is somehow defective, it is vacated—that is, eliminated—and either a substitute order is entered or a new hearing is granted, which will ultimately result in a new order, judgment, or decree.

WITHOUT PREJUDICE   Orders, judgments, and decrees that are entered without prejudice can be modified at a later time without the necessity of proving a material change in circumstances justifying the modification. Orders are normally entered without prejudice by agreement rather than as a result of a court hearing.

BIBLIOGRAPHY

DIVORCE (SPECIFIC GROUNDS, EXAMPLES, PSYCHOLOGICAL, FINANCIAL)

Between Love and Hate: A Guide to Civilized Divorce. Lois Gold. New York: Plenum Publishing Corp., 1992.

Coping: A Survival Manual for Women Alone. Martha Yates. Englewood Cliffs, N.J.: Prentice-Hall, 1976.

Creative Divorce: A New Opportunity for Personal Growth. Mel Krantzler. New York: M. Evans, 1974.

The Custody Handbook. Persia Woolley. New York: Summit Books, 1979.

The Custody Trap: Helping Children of Divorce. June and William Noble. New York: Hawthorn Books, 1975.

Dealing with Divorce. Robert K. Moffett and Jack F. Scherer. Boston: Little, Brown, 1976.

Divorce and Decision-Making. Christina Robertson. Chicago: Follett, 1979.

The Divorce Book/for Men and Women: A Step by Step Guide to Gaining Your Freedom Without Losing Everything Else. Harriet Newman Cohen and Ralph Gardner, Jr. New York: Avon Books, 1994.

The Divorce Experience. Bernice and Morton Hunt. New York: McGraw-Hill, 1977.

Divorce: A Four Letter Word. Peter L. Grieco, Michael J. Termini, and Mark M. Grieco. West Palm Beach, FL: Pt Publications, 1993.

Divorce Help Sourcebook. Margorie Engel. Detroit: Gale Research, 1994.

Divorce: The Man's Complete Guide to Winning. Lauren O. Vail. New York: Sovereign Books, 1979.

Everything You Want to Know About Your Husband's Money . . . & Need to Know Before the Divorce. Shelley Aspaklaria and Gerson Geltner. New York: T. Y. Crowell, 1980.

The Fighter's Guide to Divorce. Robert Blackwell. Chicago: Regnery, 1977.

Getting Custody: Winning the Last Battle of a Marital War. Robert H. Woody. New York: Macmillan, 1978.

How to Divorce Your Wife. Fordin Athearn. New York: Nordon Pubns., 1977.

How to Get Out of an Unhappy Marriage. Eugene Walder. New York: Putnam, 1978.

Marital Separation. Robert S. Weiss. New York: Basic Books, 1975.

No-Fault Divorce. Michael A. Wheeler. Boston: Beacon Press, 1974.

The Trouble with Lawyers. Murray Teigh Bloom. New York: Simon & Schuster, 1969.

Uncoupling. Norman Sheresky and Marya Mannes. New York: Viking Press, 1972.

What Every Man Should Know About Divorce. Robert Cassidy. Washington, D.C.: New Republic Books, 1977.

CHILDREN AND DIVORCE

The Best Interests of the Child: The Least Detrimental Alternative. Joseph Goldstein (ed.), Albert J. Solnit, and Sonja Goldstein. New York: Free Press, 1996.

The Boys and Girls Book About Divorce. Richard A. Gardner. New York: Bantam, 1971.

Child Custody. James C. Black and Donald J. Cantor. New York: Columbia University Press, 1989.

Child Custody: Building Agreements That Work. Mimi E. Lyster. Berkeley, CA: Nolo Press, 1996.

The Custody Revolution: The Father Factor and the Motherhood Mystique. Richard A. Warshak. New York: Simon & Schuster, 1992.

Divorce and Child Custody: Your Options and Legal Rights. Deanna Peters and Richard L. Strohm. Hawthorne, NJ: Career Press, Inc., 1994.

Mothers on Trial: The Battle for Children and Custody. Phyllis Chesler. New York: Harcourt Brace & Co., 1991.

Reinventing the Family: The Emerging Story of Lesbian and Gay Parents. Laura Benkov, Ph.D. New York: Random House Value Publishers, 1993.

Renegotiating Family Relationships: Divorce, Child Custody and Mediation. Robert E. Emery. New York: Guilford Press, 1994.

Talking About Divorce: A Dialogue Between Parent & Child. Earl A. Grollman. Boston: Beacon Press, 1975.

What Every Child Would Like Parents to Know About Divorce. Lee Salk. New York: Harper & Row, 1978.

About the Author

JAMES T. FRIEDMAN is a specialist in family law and practices with the firm of Davis, Friedman, Zavett, Kane & MacRae in Chicago. In addition to his private practice, he has drafted family law–related legislation on behalf of the Illinois State Bar Association, the Chicago Bar Association, and the American Academy of Matrimonial Lawyers. He has been the chairman of the Chicago Bar Association Family Law Committee and Illinois State Bar Association Family Law Council and is a member of the Family Law Section of the American Bar Association. Mr. Friedman is past president of the American Academy of Matrimonial Lawyers. He was the author, editor, and publisher of the *Illinois Family Law Report* and has written many articles for legal journals on divorce, child custody, and other related matters. Mr. Friedman lives in Chicago with his wife, Carolyn. The Friedmans have three children: a daughter, who is an artist living in California, and two sons, who practice law in Chicago.

About the Type

This book was set in Electra, a typeface designed for Linotype by W. A. Dwiggins, the renowned type designer (1880–1956). Electra is a fluid typeface, avoiding the contrasts of thick and thin strokes that are prevalent in most modern typefaces.